SPARE A COPPER!

SPARE A COPPER!

DICK KENYON

with cartoons by Larry

JAVELIN BOOKS
LONDON · NEW YORK · SYDNEY

First published in the UK 1987 by Blandford Press.
This Javelin Books edition first published 1988
Artillery House, Artillery Row, London SW1P 1RT

Distributed in the United States by
Sterling Publishing Co, Inc,
2 Park Avenue, New York, NY 10016

Distributed in Australia by
Capricorn Link (Australia) Pty Ltd
P O Box 665, Lane Cove, NSW 2066

British Library Cataloguing in Publication Data

Kenyon, Dick
Spare a copper.
1. London. Police : Metropolitan Police -
Personal observations
I. Title
363.2'092'4

ISBN 0 7137 2050 6

Printed in Great Britain by Cox & Wyman Ltd,
Reading, Berks.

CONTENTS

CHAPTER 1

As I felt the first arrow strike home, my hand flashed towards my hip, but before I could draw my weapon, four more arrows had found their mark and I slumped to the ground in the doorway. The Indians stepped over my prostrate body and, with muffled yells and laughter, disappeared into the half-light in search of their next victim.

The year was 1956 and I had been posted to Ryford some six months previously. Twelve miles from the centre of London, it was a typical suburban town. The main shopping area was centred around the High Street, which was nearly a mile long. In their wisdom the powers that be had decided that this high-risk area should be policed by splitting it into three foot patrols with three other beats superimposed on these. In this way the most vulnerable part of the town would receive maximum coverage. To avoid any chance of leaving the area unpoliced at change-over times, the wireless cars and the High Street started and finished an hour later than the beat duty men.

Even though I knew I must complete two years probation before I could apply to be allowed to specialise as a dog-handler, which was the ambition which had led me to join the police force in the first place, I had thought that the job would offer more excitement than it had so far. The price I paid for being the newest probationer was a regular posting to one of the High Street patrols whenever I was on night duty. The police day was basically divided into three shifts or reliefs: early turn, from 6 am to 2 pm; late turn, from 2 pm to 10 pm;

and night duty. In a nine-week cycle, an officer would be on alternate late and early turns for six weeks and do three weeks continuous night duty. Night duty in a town which was dead after midnight was boredom at its highest.

Coming on duty that night, I had shaken hands with all the shop door-handles, been available when the pubs turned out and supervised the closing of the late-night café. Then, as usual, I had window-shopped and generally passed the time away. It was always the same routine and I was not alone in my boredom: all other patrols and beatmen suffered in the same way. That was until two tours of night duty prior to this one when, in general conversation immediately before starting duty, it was decided that the men should split into two groups and that from 1 am each night they should become cowboys and Indians. Within reason there were few rules except that no one would attack whilst the Duty Inspector or Sergeant was in the area.

This had been the fourth night in succession that I had been ambushed and " killed". The Indians always had the advantage as they were able to make bows and arrows by raiding the local park and using the canes that the gardeners used for supporting the flowers; all a cowboy could do was draw his truncheon and pretend it was a revolver.

When I arrived back at the station I was met by gloating faces and general taunting. I vowed there and then that sooner or later I would take my revenge, but especially on the "chief" of the Indians, PC 2202 William Evans: pest, practical joker, possessor of a weird sense of humour, and someone you could never rely upon to do anything except to organise chaos from the smallest incident. Many were the officers who had nearly ended up in trouble because of Bill Evans. His idea of fun was to make someone look an idiot in public. Like the time when he was off duty and saw a fellow officer, PC Tony Yorke, struggling with a very unwilling stray dog on a piece of string. He immediately crossed the road and started to rant and rave at Tony Yorke, accusing him of stealing the dog, taking it for vivisection, cruelty etc. Then, when a crowd had formed and were accusing the officer of all manner of things, Bill Evans just disappeared. On another occasion he successfully convinced a very young probationer PC that a hearse waiting for a coffin to be brought out of a house was causing an obstruction and that the driver should be reported. By the time the probationer reached the hearse, Bill Evans was nowhere to be seen. Should anything ever happen to Bill Evans,

the list of suspects with grudges would be a mile long. Sooner or later he would suffer retribution. For myself, an idea had been forming in my mind ever since my first "killing" and I decided to implement it at the very first opportunity.

My police career had begun in the quadrangle in the centre of the Metropolitan Police Training School, Peel House, Regency Street, Westminster, London. Why was I there? All because of a film at the local cinema a year before. Recently married, my wife and I had gone to see the film, "The Blue Lamp", starring Jack Warner – a film which inspired more people to join the police force than any official recruiting film could have done. I have no idea why, but something stirred in me as I watched it. I had always loved animals and in particular dogs. How wonderful it would be, I had thought, to train to become a police dog-handler, with all the excitement that being a policeman must bring. It was silly to contemplate giving up a good, secure job as a post office telecommunications engineer, a job in which I had served a full apprenticeship before having to do my National Service and to which I had returned when the two years were completed. Yet as hard as I tried, I could not get rid of the feeling that working with a police dog was all that I wanted to do. In the end, my wife and I had a long discussion about it. We decided that I should apply to join the police force and see what happened. To my surprise, I passed the entrance examinations and was offered a place on a course starting in June. By now my enthusiasm had become an ambition so strong that I knew I could not ignore it, so after much soul-searching, we agreed that I should accept. Now here I was, standing in the parade quadrangle with my suitcase by my side, along with thirty-nine other entrants.

"PARADE!" The Drill Sergeant's command rattling round the quadrangle brought me sharply back to the present.

"Parade, Atten-n-n-shun!" It was obvious that all of the men on parade had served in His Majesty's Armed Forces, for they snapped to attention as one. A senior officer, who we later found out was of the rank of Superintendent, climbed the stone steps which served as a dais and began his welcoming speech. "Work hard, no time for relaxing in the local public houses, etc, etc. Space here is very limited, so all of you whose surnames begin with the letters A to L stand fast, you will undergo training here. Those whose surnames begin with the letters M to Z will, on command, fall out and embark on the coach which is waiting outside the front of the building. You will undergo training at Hendon. A to L stand fast; M to Z fall out."

How pleased I was that my name began with K. This meant that I was to do my training at Peel House, which was only ten minutes walk from Victoria Station and the main-line railway service to my home town. It was only a further five minutes walk home, whereas Hendon was North London and it would have taken nearly two hours to get home each Saturday lunch time. After all, with a three-month-old baby, living in a town 200 miles away from her home village, life was not going to be easy for my wife, Janet. In spite of the rail strike which had been going on for about a week, a few trains were running and if necessary I could get home in the evenings as well as weekends.

"At the double, form three ranks in a line with the white lines on the wall of the building," came the next order from the Drill Sergeant. Those of us left in the quadrangle formed up. As if from nowhere, five sergeants appeared in front of us. "These are your course instructors. They will take you to your rooms and then to your first lecture. Over to you, instructors," said the Drill Sergeant.

The course instructors wasted no time and within an hour we were all seated in a classroom ready for our first lecture. So started thirteen weeks of practical and theoretical instruction in all aspects of policing: accidents, courts, disturbances, drunks, illness in the street, dead bodies, indecency, prostitution, bookmakers etc: all those things which were so strange to us then, but which we would eventually discover to be everyday occurrences in the London police force.

It is strange, those features which stick in your mind about training school after all these years. The most vivid and the most horrible for me was the smell and sight of cold boiled eggs and just warm porridge which was left out for breakfast every Monday morning for those of us who had gone home for the weekend.

Most of us found that the only way to learn the mass of Acts, Powers of Arrest, procedures and definitions required of us was by rote. This meant that virtually every spare moment was taken up with trying to learn something. Student constables were to be found everywhere, instruction books in hand, eyes closed, mumbling to themselves. Then we would re-read whatever it was and recite it over and over again. Strangely, it became easier as the course progressed. Not because there was less to learn – quite the contrary, every day the list got longer – but because your brain became used to being worked in this way and it then readily accepted more and more information. However, in the early stages all manner of things got mixed up. One afternoon during the second week the Superintendent entered the room and snapped questions at whoever happened to be closest to him.

"What are the primary objects?" he snapped at the woman recruit in the front row.

"Er...um... the primary objects of an efficient police force are first to travel from town to town and other men's houses, with a blue light flashing on the top of your helmet," came the reply before the poor girl had time to stop herself.

The whole course collapsed with laughter, as did the instructor. The Superintendent did not. "You've got at least four different definitions bloody well mixed up there. Learn them all properly by the morning or you'll be off the course. Bloody women. Why they ever let them in the job, I'll never know." He went off into a tirade of swearing and abuse, which very quickly reduced the poor girl to tears. On leaving the room, he slammed the door so hard behind him that it was a wonder the glass did not shatter. When things had calmed down, the instructor told the student not to worry because he happened to know that the Superintendent was going on two weeks annual leave the next day.

This outburst, we discovered later, was typical of this strange and rather coarse man. He claimed at the end of the course that it was all part of the teaching process, to get us used to the kind of reactions we would meet on the street. However, I do not think that he ever convinced any student that this was his only motive for his attitude.

In retrospect, though, I can see that most of the pressure was designed to enable us to pick out the right definition or Power of Arrest at a moment's notice when confronted with it in the streets. In practice, very little survived when you were on the beat. Ninety per cent of police work is done on instinct, and you hope that your immediate actions when confronted with an incident are confirmed as correct when the books are studied at the station afterwards.

Not just theory was taught but practical training was also given, with the instructors playing the public. There were those who acted the part of the meek and mild and admitted everything or were helpful to a fault. There were the aggressive types, both verbally and physically, the unco-operative types and those who suffered from either mental or physical handicaps or both, plus loving or aggressive drunks: all types which we would meet in the streets when we got out there. These staged incidents not only taught us how to deal with such characters but also revealed the short-tempered, violent or easily upset students: more failed the course for these reasons than for any other.

It was all done very subtly, but every one of us was put to the test several times during the course. We all claimed that the instructors played their parts to excess, and that it could never happen on the streets. How wrong could we be? Those instructors were like cuddly toys in comparison to what the public were actually like. There was no wonder that we were pressed or pushed way past any point that we had ever reached before. One of our number, Taffy Williams, had stood up to the course well and was on one of the numerous practical examinations which were set at regular intervals through the course. This one involved personal injury caused in a road traffic accident. In this incident, the set-up was that a pedal cyclist had turned without warning or any signals in front of a bus, which had hit the cyclist. The cyclist was drunk and was now slowly becoming aggressive.

"Now, now, calm down, sir. I will give you the name of the bus driver and the address of London Transport so that you can claim direct to them about your damaged cycle," said Taffy.

"I want damages here and now," slurred the cyclist, poking Taffy forcibly in the chest.

"That is not possible, sir. You have to claim later, by letter, if you want damages," replied Taff.

"Don't give me that claptrap, I demand payment now," said the cyclist, thrusting his face towards Taff's and emphasising each word by poking him hard in the chest with the forefinger of his right hand. "Right" – poke – "now" – poke.

Taff was beginning to lose control of the situation. Slowly he was being driven backwards across the yard, further and further away from the scene of the accident. "I would suggest you stop that before I arrest you for assaulting a police officer."

"A" – poke – "what?" – poke – "A" – poke – "police officer?" – poke – "A" – poke – "police" – poke – "officer?" – poke – "Don't" – poke – "make" – poke – "me" – poke – "laugh."

All the time this was taking place, the cyclist was pretending to drink from a bottle of whisky and was continually emphasising each word by poking his finger hard into Taff's chest. "You're nothing else than a stupid Welsh bastard."

This was too much for Taff. He went berserk. Grabbing the drunk cyclist by the hair, he punched him in the face. The instructor fell to the ground, blood pouring from his nose. Taffy was screaming at him, "Welsh I may be, but bastard I am not!" He then ran off into the training school, sobbing.

"Constable Kenyon, what rights does Section 66 of the Metropolitan Police Act give you?" I stood up slowly, collecting my thoughts. "Section, er, 66 of the Metropolitan Police...." My voice trailed off. From my vantage point standing up, I was able to see out of the window, down into Regency Street. There I saw the very dejected figure of Taffy Williams in plain clothes, carrying his suitcase and walking slowly in the direction of the railway station.

When at last the course was finished, we were given a week's leave

to recover, then posted to our respective Section. My ambition to transfer eventually to the Police Dog Branch was as strong as ever, but I knew that I had to learn all the basics of good policing first, during my two years as a probationer. I was lucky because I was posted for those two years to my home town of Ryford.

I was lucky in another way, because on the very first day that I was posted late turn (2 pm to 10 pm), I was partnered with a really old-time copper by the name of Sam Miller. "Dusty" had joined the force in 1928, five years before I was even born. He was the "Father" of the nick and was treated with respect from the highest to the lowest. I was proud to have been posted with him. Unlike many old-time coppers, Dusty was only too willing to pass on the benefit of his years of experience to any young policeman who was willing to listen.

Although he would never realise it, I had had a great deal of respect, if not apprehension, for "Mr Miller" since I was thirteen years old. It was then that he had caught me climbing over the fence out of Danes House Orchard, with my pockets full of pears. "Got you, m'lad," said Dusty, taking hold of a handful of left ear. "Now what am I going to do with you, eh?"

"Don't know, sir," I had said in a very weak and trembling voice whilst standing on tiptoes.

"Now, let's see, I could take you to court and have you sent to

prison for the rest of your life, or-r-r, on the other hand, I could take you home for your Dad to deal with you, or-r-r, I could take you up to the big house and make you apologise. Now, which one shall it be?"

"Please sir..." but before I could continue, there came the command, "Right, empty out your pockets. Now my name is Mr Miller and you remember to call me that in the future, understand?"

"Yes sir, Mr Miller, sir".

Crack! Crack! My legs were struck one after the other in very quick succession by an expertly wielded rolled-up police cape. "Right, clear off and don't let me catch you again, m'lad."

"Yes sir, I mean, no sir, Mr Miller, sir," I replied as I ran off rubbing each leg in turn, like a stork with arthritis. Now here I was, proudly walking number one beat with that same Mr Miller.

"What would you say to a cup of tea, eh, lad?"

"Fine by me, Dusty, but how can we go back to the station already?"

"Well, lad, there's stations and stations. Follow me." With that he turned into the entrance of Ryford railway station.

He stopped, turned round and stood with his legs slightly apart, hands behind his back. "Always check that the Section Sergeant or the Duty Officer is nowhere near before going in anywhere," he said.

Five minutes later we entered the booking office. " 'Allo, another new face. What's your name? Mine's Albert."

"I'm Dick. Pleased to meet you." This watering-hole was to serve many purposes in the years to come, I discovered.

Otherwise, the first half of that tour of duty was uneventful. Dusty pointed out one or two of the local "boys" who sailed close to the wind in respect of keeping on the right side of the law. We chatted amicably until "grub time". When we arrived at the station canteen I very soon discovered that even though I was working with him, I was not allowed to sit with Dusty at the table reserved for the old-time coppers.

Leaving the station some 45 minutes later, we strolled along in front of the shops, checking the door-handles and windows as we passed. "Soon there won't be any design of shop door or its fittings that you won't be familiar with," Dusty told me. "I've shaken hands with padlocks so large you could hardly get your hands around them or so small that if you pulled them too hard they came open in your hand. At least you can always snap those shut again. Watch out for brass door-knobs: don't grip them with your full hand so that your fingers come in contact with the inside shaft. Many is the piece of skin I've left on the holding screw which was proud of its hole. Or else you'll end up with a hole in your woollen knitted glove which either catches on the screw or gets trapped when the shaft is loose through the door."

I listened, fascinated. This was not the sort of information they gave us at training school, but it was invaluable, hard-won experience that Dusty was passing on. "And doorways," my tutor continued. "They've got more uses than you'd imagine. They give shelter from the rain or winds. They are places of observation so that if you stand in the right position, you can see any movement up and down the roadway without being seen yourself. In very cold weather it can be five to ten degrees warmer in a well-lit doorway. Others have got conveniently placed sills or ledges for sitting or resting on. Most are suitable for a quick cigarette and for keeping out of the Duty Officer's way."

"Regis's, Purveyor of High Class Groceries" read the sign across the top of one double-fronted shop in the Market Square which Dusty and I checked that night. With premises not apparently altered since it was founded in 1851, this was a fascinating shop just to stop and look at, especially in the daytime. Along the street drifted the smell of roasting coffee from a side window with a row of wooden-handled roasting cylinders slowly rotating over the low flames. The Buttery Manager would be patting and rolling the butter into half-pounds using the wooden butter bats; for special occasions he would carry out butter sculpture, creating three-foot-high swans, castles and the like, all this being performed in one of the larger windows. The Greengrocery Manager, in another large window, created his own personal masterpieces of intricate patterns or sculpture with the aid of oranges, pears, cucumbers, tomatoes and the rest of his products. These two large windows were fitted with a pair of large brass handles at the bottom of the frame from the outside. Originally there had been counters in the window, and in the summer months they were opened so that customers could be served through them. Now they could be used by the managers, especially the greengrocery manager, when they were constructing their latest creations from outside on the pavement when necessary. These windows were lockable, and as we checked them to ensure that they were in fact secured for the night, Dusty enquired "Have you had an arrest yet, lad?"

"No. I wish I could get one, it must be a wonderful feeling."

"*Never, ever* think that arresting someone is a wonderful feeling," retorted Dusty. "To take someone into custody is to deprive them of their right to walk the street as free men. You should only arrest someone when you are absolutely certain they deserve it. During your service you'll have to nick people for serious assaults which were committed for no apparent reason, for indecency to small kids and for many other offences. You'll feel the urge to take revenge on behalf of the innocent persons. Don't do it, because it will always go sour on you and you'll be in the wrong, not them."

I stood wide-mouthed, not knowing quite what to say. No-one had ever talked to me about arrests, or for that matter about any other part of police work in that way. I later learnt that Dusty had his own very strong opinions about policing in all its many forms. What may be even more important was that most of them made a lot of sense if only you took time out to think about them seriously. Having left school at 14, he had received the minimum of formal education, but was a graduate in honours of the University of Life. He was living proof that experience and natural wisdom are a combination to beat any textbook theory or dry classroom lesson.

"Right then, lecture over. Let's go and find you an arrest. Up here, lad." So saying, Dusty led the way up an alley to the rear of five shops. It was pitch-black and, without putting his torch on, he shouted out, "Right then, you two, we can see you! Stand where you are, you're under arrest."

We both listened intently, but the only sound to be heard was the traffic in the High Street. "This is the last time of telling. Either stand still or I'll send the police dog in after you," shouted Dusty. "You told me you wanted to be a dog-handler didn't you?" he whispered to me. "Now's your chance. Bark or growl or do whatever police dogs do."

"Do what?"

"Bark, you fool, or we'll lose them."

"Lose who?"

"Don't argue, do as I say."

This was it! I had been warned that old timers would try to fool me into doing something stupid and that before I even got back to the station, I would be the butt of the canteen jokers and would remain so for many weeks to come. "Oh no, you don't catch me like that," I said.

"Keep your voice down," he whispered. "We don't want them to know we haven't got a dog, do we? Are you two going to come out or not?" he added in a loud voice.

"All right, Dusty, how many of the relief are up there? More than half, I'll bet, all waiting to get a good laugh at my expense."

Before Dusty could reply, a voice came out of the darkness. "All right, mate, we give in but don't send in the dog, will yer?"

"My God, there's someone there!" exclaimed Dusty. The beams of our two torches stabbed the darkness in the general direction of the voice. Dusty's torch had seen better days and was in desperate need of new batteries. His beam ended in mid-air about five feet in front of him. More light could have been generated by rubbing two Boy Scouts together – or a Boy Scout and a Girl Guide for that matter.

My torch was new and in its beam, about twenty-five yards away, we could see two men aged about forty, one with a jemmy in his hand, standing beside a first-floor rear window of the hardware store next door to Regis's. By what I could see, they had been working on it for quite some time.

"We won't give you any trouble, guv," said the man holding the jemmy.

"Right then, Dick, you know what to say and do. Go ahead. I'll hold your torch for you so that you have both hands free," said Dusty.

"Yes! OK! Right! Here you are then!" I gasped as I handed him my torch. My mouth was dry and I was shaking slightly as I tried to remember exactly how we had been taught to do it at training school. That was it, I remembered. I stepped forward towards the men, knowing exactly what I was going to do and say. "Keep the light on them, Dusty. Here we go."

I had taken about five or six steps when suddenly the ground disappeared from under me. Before I could comprehend what was happening, I had landed with a very loud smash into the middle of the dustbins and cardboard cartons in the basement area of the shop. The noise echoed around the back of the shops, sounding as if the local demolition company was hard at work. The two shop-breakers ran down the fire-escape steps and reached me long before Dusty peered over the edge, shining my torch on the chaos below him. "Blimey! You all right, mate? We thought you had killed yourself. You keep that dog up there, we ain't going to 'urt 'im," said one of the shop-breakers.

"Yes thanks, but I've twisted my ankle," I said in a shaky voice.

"Right then, you two, help him up and we'll walk to the nick," ordered Dusty.

"OK, mate, but you keep that dog on a lead."

We made a strange sight, walking up the High Street: me hobbling along on my sprained ankle, being helped by the two shop-breakers, one of whom kept asking me, "Where's that bloody dog, I hate bleedin' dogs"; with Dusty fetching up the rear, swinging the jemmy in his right hand and saying "Heel!" every now and then. It took longer for me to live that down than if I had really been the victim of a set-up.

The following morning at court, I limped into the witness box to outline the facts to the magistrates in response to the guilty pleas that my two shop-breakers made. I also mentioned how they had come to my assistance. This, I think, saved them from going to prison and they were fined ten pounds each with time to pay. I was very proud of my first two crime arrests in spite of the fact that I had originally been convinced that I was being set up for some massive hoax. Just before he retired, Dusty confided to me that he had never known it work before that night. I can tell him now, if he is still alive, that it never worked again for me either.

Chapter 2

No matter where any police officer performs his duty, if he does so in a particular location regularly, then it is not long before he has his own private bogey area. It can be a road, a factory, a shop or a sports ground; but it is a place where more often than not, if he goes there, something happens, usually for the worse. However, the reverse is also true, luckily. My "bogey" was that "Purveyor of High Class Groceries" in Ryford's Market Square, Regis's.

This shop's big display windows at least provided special interest to the foot patrol which covered the Market Square, particularly when a new fruit and vegetable masterpiece was being created by the Greengrocery Manager. Just like Rome, they were not built in a day; depending on the subject, they could take two or three to complete. During one week, a couple of months after I had been posted to Ryford, I watched with interest the slowly forming coach and horses over the Friday and Saturday whilst I was late turn. By mid- afternoon on Saturday this latest creation was finished. Later, after the store had closed and the shoppers gone home, I stopped to have a closer look. Yes, the spokes of the wheels were made of cucumbers, and the ears of the horses were bananas. I admitted to myself that I was mildly jealous of such creative art. After all, my highly acclaimed (by myself) matchstick men were hardly in the same class.

Just as I had decided "each to their own", two noisy drinkers emerged from the public bar of the "Greyhound" pub opposite. I turned to make sure that they went on their way without creating a nuisance. Automatically I pulled upwards on one of the brass handles to make sure that all was secure. To my amazement the giant window flew upwards, aided by the hidden counter-balance weight, hit the top, stopped and shattered. Such was the force of the impact that the coach and horses also collapsed. Fruit and vegetables spilled out of the window, over the pavement and into the road, closely followed by ninety- eight square feet of plate glass.

The next two hours were a complete mystery to me. I vaguely remember the whole of the pub turning out and standing roaring with laughter; the Duty Officer's car crunching and squelching to a halt; being given a broom; and then sitting in the canteen at the station asking all the old-time coppers for advice on how to write out this report.

For many months after this I shook hands very gently with the shop door- knobs, and even more delicately with the lovely new plate-glass window in Regis's, Purveyor of High Class Groceries. That was until one night duty about six months later when Tony Yorke and I were standing in Regis's doorway, keeping very quiet observation, waiting for our next victim.

All police stations have their annual championship competitions – snooker, billiards, dominoes, checkers, etc – but few, if any, had one that could compare with Ryford's. Its origins were lost in antiquity but there was a trophy – appropriately, a stuffed version of the competition's very first victim, the one which had actually started off the whole thing. The knock-out competition was known to one and all as the "sudden death championship", the only qualifications being that the competitor was of no higher rank than constable, that the competitor was stationed at Ryford and that the champion of each relief's competition met off-duty to decide the supreme champion.

After about thirty minutes silent waiting, Tony gently nudged me and pointed to the shadows on the opposite side of the road. Slowly the object of our attention wandered out of an alley into full view. Stopping immediately in the pool of light from the street lamp, Rattus norvegicus was the perfect target; my pulse quickened as I realised that I would never have a better chance of staking my claim as champion rat-hunter. Slowly I drew my weapon from my trouser pocket, took careful aim and loosed off my shot. The lignum- vitae truncheon sped across the road, missed the sitting brown rat, struck the kerbstone and ricocheted straight through the window of the jeweller's shop opposite us.

Strangely, there were no crashing sounds of breaking glass, just a crisp, loud cracking sound. Slowly Tony and I crossed the road and found a neat hole punched in the bottom corner of the window, with the truncheon resting half in and half out of the display. It took over an hour and several trips to the local park before the correct size of stone could be located and placed in the hole. "On Tuesday, 27th February, 1956, at 3.10 am at 27 Market Square, Ryford, whilst patrolling on foot I noticed a hole about 2½ inches in diameter in the left-hand corner of the window of Royal's the jewellers. Resting just inside the window was a round stone of approximately 2 inches in diameter. I had previously examined the premises at 12.35 am and had found them to have been correct. It can therefore only be assumed that the stone had been thrown up by a passing vehicle."

Rattus norvegicus lived to be aimed at again and I was disqualified for trying to cut its throat with a piece of broken window-glass. This was judged as not being within the spirit of the competition.

It was thanks to Tony Yorke that the boiler-room of Ryford Football Club was one of our best watering-holes. Tony's father was the club's groundsman, so always had a welcome for any passing constable who might drop in during working hours. After 5 pm the end shed of the three which stood beside the pavilion could always be relied upon to have all the necessary makings of a cuppa. It was even known, on occasions, to have a football lurking away in the corner. Now, if the combination of two officers on adjoining beats visiting the shed at the same time, plus a discarded football in the corner of the shed, plus an empty football field in the middle of the night, just happened to occur, then it needs little or no imagination to realise what nearly always happened. However, if you add two visiting beat officers, one nosey neighbour who notices a torchlight and noises coming from the ground at 4 am on an August morning and the crews of two wireless cars who respond to the "suspects on premises" R/T call, then you have a three-a-side football match in progress before you can chant, "One, two, three, four, who are we for, R-Y-F-O-R-D, Ryford!" It was just my luck, on the only occasion that this happened whilst I was there, for the Duty Officer to arrive on the scene to check if indeed there were any suspects on premises. Luckily it was a Station Sergeant (a now obsolete rank) who, being recently promoted, still firmly approved of using the facilities presenting themselves. He joined in for ten minutes and then told us all off and threatened us with being placed on disciplinary report the next time.

The one place in Ryford which could literally be called a water-

ing-hole was the open-air swimming pool. Only open in the summer months, it was an ideal place to cool down on those hot, sticky nights we so often had in July and August. The problem was that there were so few truly dark hours at that time of the year, that inevitably any officer who just slipped in for a cooling dip stood the risk of being spotted from one of the surrounding houses as dawn came up.

PC Ernie "Blossom" Trevellyn was a true son of the soil. He was born in Cornwall to a ploughman and his wife. Ernie's father had worked a pair of beautiful Shire horses on the farm, and Ernie had been brought up with them. He had alo been taught how to work them. It was this teaching that Ernie had brought with him into the police force and used for all of the manoeuvres of the police vehicles he drove, just as though the highly tuned fast car was one of his beloved Shires. His "Steady there, Blossom", delivered in his rich, west-country accent, had earned him his nickname. He was as passionate about horses as I was about dogs.

Now Blossom did not like the heat, and one sweltering night in August found him and me walking adjacent beats. "How about a dip then, young Dick?" he greeted me as we met.

"Not me, I hate swimming. I wouldn't mind a shower, though, but not a swim," I replied.

"Come on then, my beauty, we can climb over the railings and have one before it gets light."

Reluctantly I agreed and within half an hour, Ernie and I were stripped off in the men's changing-rooms. Neither of us had towels but this did not matter too much as it did not take long to dry off naturally in the heat. Nor did we have trunks. After all, where would we have been able to carry all that gear?

Blossom slipped silently into the water at the deep end and, using the breast stroke because it is the quietest, swam several lengths. For my part, I went into the shower-room and enjoyed a tepid shower which I took my time over, revelling in the coolness.

"You finished then, Dick?" came the familiar voice of Blossom as he came into the shower-room. "Hey, look what I've found," he said suddenly. Before I could answer, he crossed the room, bent down and retrieved a towel from under a bench. It was not long before he started to flick at my completely naked body with the end of the towel. This hurt, and I was soon running and jumping to avoid Blossom and his deadly weapon.

"You bastard, that hurt. Knock it off, Blossom." Already I had several red weals on my backside and the tops of my legs at the front. "Stop it, Bloss, we've got to get dressed and out of here, "I said frantically.

"Just one more hit and then we'll be off," he said, at the same time running towards me.

There was no way I was stopping to get hit again. I turned and ran, bursting out of the door onto the poolside, where Ryford Swimming Club's lady coach was saying to a line of twenty-two females aged from fourteen to thirty- two, "Now it's very good of you girls to get here so early to rehearse our formation swimming routine for this Saturday's gala."

I was looking over my shoulder as I ran and it was then that I saw the first two ladies of the line that I had already run past. Blossom was so intent on hitting me that he collided with the first one as he reached her. I will always remember the remarks and laughter, especially as we got dressed and slipped out of the dressing-rooms with our hands on our shoulders to cover our numbers. In this way,

they would have to hold an identity parade if they complained. Mind you, it would have been a very interesting parade, bearing in mind which physical feature they could most readily identify, especially when by law it was necessary to obtain volunteers from the passers-by in the street to make up the line.

Chapter 3

That summer was hot, the hottest for years. So hot in fact, that when I stepped into the road the melting tar stuck to my boots. I have always hated the hot weather: snow and ice were fine by me, you could wrap up well or put on extra layers of underclothes; walk faster or flap your arms and stamp your feet. But there was no escaping heat like this, which apparently didn't change day or night. The only saving grace for me was the way in which the ladies divested themselves of most of their unwanted clothing. There were some truly beautiful sights to be seen during the hot weather, the only trouble being that they tended to raise my temperature even higher. Mind you, I have always wondered where all those curvaceous bodies go to in the winter time.

This was in the days when the Metropolitan Police had just managed to stagger forward into doing away with the dog-collar type jackets. Now we wore jackets with shirts which had detachable stiff collars. Admittedly we were issued with barathea jackets and lightweight trousers for summer use but these only served to cover the sweat-soaked shirts from the public's gaze. A far cry indeed from the present-day police uniforms with their short sleeves, open-necked shirts, no jackets, lightweight trousers and shoes. Mind you, we could get permission to wear our helmet-straps up inside the helmet to avoid a white line on the face. Police clothing has travelled a very slow and tortuous journey over the past thirty-odd years to arrive where it is today.

Slowly I walked along Common Road on the shaded side in the

direction of the police box to make my scheduled telephone call to the station. As I rounded the bend on the hill, I should be able to see if the box was in the sun or the shade. How I hoped it was in the shade, a chance to take the weight off my aching feet and to grab a quick cigarette. Even if it was in the shade you could guarantee that the confined space inside the box would be at least ten degrees higher than outside. If the box was in the sun then it would be so hot that it would be impossible even to step into it without running the risk of suffering heat exhaustion. I reached the point in the road where number 21 box should have come into view, but there was no box to be seen, just a pall of black smoke lazily drifting skyward.

I instinctively quickened my pace before I realised that it was most unlikely that a prefabricated concrete box with only a small door, stool and short bench made of wood could first of all catch fire and then create so much black smoke. As I got nearer I occasionally got glimpses of the box through the smoke. It was certainly not the source of the fire. Suddenly, from within the smoke, came strange metallic rattling and banging noises. These increased and from out of the smoke there appeared a most awesome sight. It had once been a gent's pedal cycle. This had been stripped of all extraneous parts; there were no tyres, mudguards, brakes, pedals, chain or saddle. Hanging from one side of the handlebars was a large metal bucket with holes punched in its sides. Inside the bucket I could see a fire glowing and from the top there rose thick black smoke which smelled of rubber. On the other side there hung four bulging paper carrier-bags. From the centre of the handlebars, tied on with string, was a collection of various pots and pans including an enormous frying pan. These bounced off the bare rim of the front wheel and threatened to become entangled with what few spokes there were left in it. Resting on top of the handlebars was a battered suitcase tied together with thick string, the contents hanging out of both ends. Astride the crossbar was a headless overcoat. There were two arms protruding from the torn sleeves and two legs coming out of the bottom but no head. On the end of each arm was what appeared to be a small bundle of rags into which disappeared the ends of the handlebars. On the end of the legs were two left shoes, one brown, one black, the sole of each shoe being attached to the upper by means of a piece of string tied around the whole shoe. From the toe of the shoe on the right foot protruded five bare and almost black toes, whilst the torn stitching on the heel of the shoe on the left foot revealed an equally bare, black heel. The trousers were torn in many

places and had string tied around them about six inches above the bottoms. Below the trousers were two inches of ankle, sporting on one leg a red sock and on the other a blue. Bouncing along behind, attached to the frame of the "cycle" by a length of rope, was an old pram chassis.

The contraption gathered speed as it came down the hill, the feet of the headless overcoat scraping along the roadway. Suddenly, the air being forced through the holes caused the bucket to burst into flames. Flames licked backwards over the left leg and the side of the overcoat. As it passed me, the contraption must have been travelling at about ten miles per hour. By this time, the pram chassis was just about to overtake the "cycle". Forty yards further, it did just that. The resulting crash could be heard for miles. Pieces of flaming rubber were scattered everywhere and within seconds the contents of the pram chassis burst into flames. The headless overcoat rolled across the road and crashed into a lamp-post, where it came to rest.

I rushed back down the road and crossed over to the overcoat. As I got close, the unmistakable stench of a meths drinker hit me. So strong was it that it made me gasp. This, mixed with the smell of stale urine and a body which had not been washed for months, along with all the attendant lodgers, both of the hopping and the sticking kind, made for a very unwelcome interruption on this sweltering afternoon.

From the depths of the overcoat came the sound of singing. "If you were the only girl in Tipperary, it's a long way to go, with me old cock linnet," came the slurred voice.

"Are you all right, are you hurt?" I shouted from a respectful distance.

The singing stopped. Slowly the bundle of rags pulled at the string around the middle of the overcoat, it came undone and the coat fell open. As it did so, a cloud of flies buzzed angrily into the air. Three more strings were tugged and pulled and three more coats of various descriptions fell open. With each one, the number of flies increased dramatically. As the last coat fell away, it revealed the body of a man clad in newspaper and string. This positive identification of the thing's gender was made easier by the holes in the pink paper of the Financial Times.

"Are you all right?" I shouted again.

At this a filthy grey hairball with a mouth somewhere in the middle of it appeared from out the newspapers. "Young man," said a slightly slurred but well-educated voice, "I will have you know – hic – that Major Joseph Petigue Smythe-Fanshaw, MC is uninjured, and is – hic – as well as can be expected in the circum – circum – hic – circumstances. I am dreadfully sorry about all the mess. I will have my man clear it away immed – immed – hic – immediat – hic – ely."

I instantly realised that Major Joseph Petigue Smythe-Fanshaw, MC was drunk - there are no flies on me, though there were millions on him. If I wanted to become the most unpopular officer stationed at Ryford, then I must obey the letter of the law and make an arrest. However, I vaguely remembered hearing somewhere that rules, regulations and laws are made for the compliance of fools and the direction of wise men. "Right then, if you're sure you are all right, I'll leave you to clear up this mess." So saying, I hastily retreated back up the hill into the refuge of the shaded police box. From there I watched out of the small glass window, to see if he did in fact clear up the road. He did.

Whilst I watched, I realised that Major Joseph Petigue Smythe-Fanshaw, MC had done it to me again: he had frightened me. This time it was the thought of having to strip and search him, if I arrested him. However, on the previous occasions it had been the fright of a boy and a young teenager who is confronted with the strange and unknown, a bogeyman in fact. Major Joseph Petigue Smythe-Fanshaw, MC, or "Smokey Joe" as he was known to most of the populace for miles around, was in fact a very sad victim of the inane trench-fighting of the First World War. "Smokey" had won his Military Cross during the fighting at Ypres. He had then been caught in a gas attack and had also been shell-shocked. After his discharge, he had taken to living rough. In 1937 his parents were killed in an avalanche in Switzerland and he inherited an estate in Norfolk, along with many thousands of pounds. Although he was traced by the executors and given hospital treatment, within three months of his release from that hospital, he was back on the road.

"Smokey" was a legend to generations of children who abused him, mocked him, stoned him, spat at him and made him suffer the hundreds of other indignities that the evil minds of children are able to devise. For all these years, he had never been known to retaliate other than by roaring like an enraged bull or pulling funny faces. His most serious offence was committed in 1942 when he saw a squad of Free Belgian soldiers in the outskirts of Ryford, when they got out of a lorry whilst a wheel was being changed. He tied a table-knife to a stick and made a bayonet charge on them, screaming "Kill the Boche!" He wounded five before he was disarmed.

"Smokey" carried all he possessed in the world with him. If there was too much to fit in the baggage, he wore it no matter what the weather. The reason for the headless overcoat was that he knew that the bucket would burst into flames; it always did. Knowing that the flames would be big enough to set fire to his hair and head, he naturally buried his head in the overcoat when going downhill and peered through a gap in the front of the coat. Why he didn't die from heat-stroke when wearing all those coats and newspapers, no-one knows. It was to be many years before "Smokey Joe" would parade in front of the Pearly Gates.

Watching "Smokey", I remembered a conversation with "Dusty" Miller in the police box a few weeks earlier. "Never forget, lad," he had said, "You're not here to stop people doing what they want to do. Some people may not fit in with what most of us think of as normal behaviour, but as long as they're not either breaking the law or making a nuisance of themselves, they're just the ones who need our protection the most. And," he added, emphasising his point by jabbing his pipe stem in my direction, "because they're treated as misfits, they're usually lonely. Being lonely is one of the worst things that can happen to a human being, and it's what "the job" is all about, being a lif-line to those people who need our help the most."

Not for the first time, nor the last, I wondered at Dusty's instinctive wisdom. I knew that he had been married for years and was surrounded by loving children and grandchildren: perhaps it was just that good fortune which gave him an insight into how a policeman should handle a problem like "Smokey Joe." He was certainly right about loneliness, which is maybe the most common form of mental illness in the world. I have no doubt the experts would tell me that it is not a mental illness in itself, only a contributing factor, but whichever is true, there can be no argument over the fact that it is loneliness which causes many sufferers to do many strange things. These vary from coming out of a house or flat and talking to anyone who passes, to long and complicated alleged wrong-doings by imaginary children, animals and adults; in fact anything which will result in getting someone to talk to them. Strangely, it is not just old people who suffer. It is also estimated that most suicides, as well as the half-hearted attempts or threats to commit suicide, are also as a direct result of loneliness.

Another of Ryford's lonely people was as much a victim of the Second World War as "Smokey" was of the First. Nellie Bradshaw had never recovered from that day in 1941 when a telegram had informed her that her husband, a Chief Petty Officer on HMS Hood, had gone down with his ship when it was sunk by the Bismarck. Since then she had let herself go and had become more and more eccentric. She seemed to divide her time between caring for all the neighbourhood's cats and complaining at Ryford police station about a man peeping in at her bedroom window.

My own first contact with Nellie Bradshaw was one misty October night, as I slowly made my way back to my High Street patrol after my refreshment period (in police language, "grub time"). As I rounded the corner into Market Square, I just glimpsed a shadowy figure disappearing into the alleyway which led to the rear of the shops. I stopped dead in my tracks, my pulse quickened and the adrenalin rushed to my brain. This was it, I thought, my first solo crime arrest. As quietly as possible I crept to the alleyway, making sure that the strap of my truncheon was clear of my pocket, just in case I needed it. Just short of the entrance I paused, so that I was not silhouetted against the street lights. Listening very intently, I could just make out the sound of movement and of whispered voices. What should I do? Should I enter the alleyway and try to find the suspects behind the shops, or wait for them to come out into the roadway? I longed for the reassuring presence of Dusty Miller beside me, as he had been on the only previous occasion I had made an arrest. My brain raced, searching for some forgotten instruction received at the training school. Nothing! Not a single instruction, direction or experience came to mind. I could not even think of telephoning for assistance, such was my excitement.

My mind was made up. I must go in after them, no matter how many there were. Slowly I crept down the alleyway towards the rear of the shops, feeling my way along with my back to the eight-foot-high boundary wall which separated the alley and the shops from the garden of the doctor's surgery. Stopping every few paces to listen intently, trying to establish the exact location and number of my shop-breakers, I heard the sound of paper and cartons being quietly moved, and a muffled voice. I waited for the sounds to stop before moving on. I had almost reached the end of the alleyway just before it turned right behind the shops. My mind was racing over what I should do and what I might find. My mouth was dry and the palms of my hands were sweating in spite of the cold. Then came another noise. This time it was the sound of a dustbin being moved. There was no turning back now. I gripped my torch tighter and prepared to step out into the open behind the shops. I took one step and then it happened: the blow came from apparently nowhere, glancing off the side of my helmet onto my shoulder and slicing open the side of my left cheek as it passed. My heart stopped in sheer terror and it felt as if it had shot up into my mouth. My breath came in short gasps and there was the strangest feeling in my stomach. Suddenly I was aware of an involuntary noise coming from my mouth as I ran back to the

Market Square and the comparative safety of the street lamps.

I leant trembling against a shop window, gasping for air and feeling the warm blood running down my face. I realised that the blow had been quite light but there must have been a nail or something similar in whatever the criminal had used to hit me to have sliced my face like that. Where he had come from and gone to, I had no idea. I had had only a glimpse of a black mass as it had descended on me. The feeling of fear slowly turned to anger. There was no way they were going to get away with this, I thought, as I attempted to get some kind of co-ordination into my limbs. I was going in after them and God help the one I laid hands on. Bracing myself, I drew my truncheon and was just about to rush into the alley when I heard a voice and shuffling footsteps coming along it towards me.

"You naughty Timmy, you know you shouldn't stay out all night. I'm getting too old to 'ave to come out looking for you. Naw I've got yer, we'll go 'ome and Mummy will give you a nice saucer of warm milk and bit of that fish I bought for you yesterday. I always know where you'll be, though, don't I? You shouldn't have done that to the nice policeman. Fancy jumping off the wall on him like that. I just don't know what I am going to do with you." Slowly a short, plump, shabbily dressed woman of about sixty-five emerged from the alleyway, holding a large black cat. "Oh, there you are, Mr Policeman. I do 'ope my Timmy didn't startle you too much. 'E's quite naughty at times, but very friendly really. Would you like to stroke 'im?"

"No, no, he didn't frighten me, madam," I heard myself saying as I slipped my truncheon back into my pocket. "What are you doing behind the shops?"

"I went to find my Timmy. 'E always gets frightened and runs away when the peeping Tom comes round my 'ouse. Do you know, 'e comes every other night and watches me take me clothes orf." As I dabbed my face with my handkerchief, Nellie said, "Oh! I do so 'ope 'e ain't 'urt yer, Mr Policeman."

"I caught it on a rose bush earlier today and it just won't stop bleeding," I lied.

"Good night then, officer. I would get a plaster on that face of yours if I was you," and off she shuffled.

"Good night, and you keep away from the back of the shops in the middle of the night in future," I responded in the most officious voice I could muster.

Nellie waddled on for about thirty yards, turned and with a rare twinkle in her eyes said, "I'd get a clean pair of underpants as well, while you're at it." Chuckling to herself, she turned to go on her way but not before I swear I saw a grin spread over the cat's face as well.

Nellie Bradshaw was to become well known to me, as she was to all the officers on the Ryford force. She became more and more eccentric, and it was inevitable that soon she would need more help than we could give her by pretending to note down her reports of missing cats and complaints about peeping Toms. One day I was passing the shabby three-floored Victorian house where she lived when she called to me, "Officer, giz an 'and. It's me lodger. I can't get any reply from 'is room and the door is locked, in't it?"

Not again! I thought, but was prepared to spend a few minutes humouring Nellie. "When did you last see him?" I asked in a resigned voice.

"Last night, arter 'e got home from the pub," came the reply.

"All right then, luv, let's see what's going on."

"Follow me," she said and led me up the short path to the front door. As we entered the hall, the smell of cats was overpowering.

Dust was everywhere, and floated in the weak winter sunshine which shafted down through the stained-glass window halfway up the first flight of stairs. "Up 'ere, two floors up, follow me," said Nellie. As we climbed the stairs, she suddenly started giggling. "I'm ever so sorry for giggling, officer, but I just remembered what 'appened the last time I walked up these stairs with a young fellah. 'E was about your age and in uniform as well. Still, that was way back at the beginning of the war when me husband was away in the Navy. God! I shouldn't tell you that, should I?" she simpered, clasping her hand to her mouth, and she giggled again as the memory of that time over fifteen years ago came flooding back to her. As she walked up the stairs in front of me, it was noticeable how, quite suddenly, her rear end developed a suggestive sway to it "'Ere's 'is room. George, George, open the bloody door!" she shouted, banging on the door with a clenched fist. There was no answer.

"Right. Before we go any further, tell me a bit about him, like how old is he? What's his job? Are you sure he's not gone out without you knowing?"

"Well, 'is name's George Phipps, 'e's been with me for eight years and 'e's about sixty. 'e couldn't have gone out without me knowing 'cause 'e always brings me a cuppa before 'e goes, don't 'e."

"Right, let me see, then," I said. I went to the door and knocked on it, bent down and listened and peeked through the keyhole. I could neither hear nor see anything. "Have you got a spare key for this door?" I asked hopefully. After all, it was one of those big, thick, heavy Victorian doors with a round brass knob-handle. The last thing I wanted to have to do was to try and shoulder the door open or attempt to kick it in. Past experience had taught me that it was all very well in films, but in practice you ended up with either a dislocated shoulder or an impacted fracture of the knee-cap.

"Naw, sorry mate, I ain't," came the dreaded reply.

"Do you mind if I force an entry into the room?" I asked. "Remember, I will cause quite a bit of damage to the door and frame if I do."

"Can't you get in through the winder? 'E always 'as it slightly open at nights, no matter what the weather," Nellie said.

"How can I get through the window? We're at the top of the house."

"Oh, that ain't no problem. 'Is winder is right above the fire escape. I'll show you. Follow me."

Now if I had been a bit quicker on the uptake or had been paying just a little more attention, I would have noticed the word "above" which was included in her suggestion.

"We can save going all the way downstairs. Come through this way, mate," Nellie said as she led the way down one flight of stairs and opened the door into what was obviously her bedroom. Immediately she burst into almost uncontrollable giggles which she tried to suppress by clasping her hands over her mouth. This time there was no explanation forthcoming, just a knowing look over the top of her fingers.

For my part, I concentrated on the job in hand. The window in the bedroom consisted of a very large sash window with a fixed-pane window on either side. On opening it, I found a metal fire-escape landing immediately outside. I climbed out, but to my dismay I found that the escape ended here. "Where's the rest of it gone?" I asked.

"Oh, I forgot, it got damaged in the bombing and they 'ad to cut the top section orf as it was dangerous, weren't it?" came the reply.

"OK, but how do I get from here to George's window?" I enquired.

"Can't yer reach the sill and pull yerself up?"

"I'm five feet ten, and with my arms stretched up I suppose I can reach about seven foot. Even if I stood on the railings I would still be a good foot short of his window-sill," I exclaimed in a slightly exasperated voice.

" 'Old on, I know," came the voice from within the room. I stood on the fire escape, staring up at the window above and trying to work out the best thing to do. Suddenly from inside the room came a banging and clattering and the sound of breaking china. "Sod the bloody thing," exclaimed the woman's voice.

I bent down, parted the curtains with my right hand and put my right leg forward to re-enter the room. As I did so I was hit in the unmentionables with the sharp end of a step-ladder. "There y'are, use this," she said.

"Thanks," I gasped, wiping a tear from my eye.

Now, heights and me are non-starters. As it was, the fact that I was out there at all was only due to sheer bravado on my part. The thought of me thirty feet above the ground on the top of a fire escape was bad enough but on top of a step-ladder as well!

"Come on, I'll hold it whilst you climb up or if you're scared, I'll go up," she said. There can be no better way of ensuring that a man does something, no matter how dangerous it may be, than by a woman who is over twice his age offering to do it for him. All my instincts screamed at me to let her do it, but manly pride and chauvinism could never allow that, although the prospect terrified me. After quite a struggle, all three of us, me, Nellie and the step-ladder, were perched dangerously on the top landing of the fire escape. We opened the steps and set them in the best position and then slowly, very slowly, I climbed them, clinging to the top rung until my feet and hands almost met and then clawing desperately at the brickwork to draw myself into an upright position.

My head and shoulders were now above the window-sill. I tried to peer through the window but the curtains were drawn. However, Nellie was right, the top window was open by about a foot. "Hold tight, luv, I'll try pushing the window up," I shouted.

"That's no good, it's nailed up. He did it 'cause it rattled in the wind. You'll have to go through the top one," she yelled back at me.

Hell, I thought. Being up there with trembling knees and able to pull myself directly through the window would have been bad enough, but to have to climb even higher was a terrifying prospect. "OK, I'll try. Hold on very tight."

Slowly I stretched up with my left hand towards the top of the open window, supporting myself with my right hand on the sill. Suddenly there was a scream of "Look out!" from below me and at the same time the steps disappeared from under my feet. Terror gripped me. I pushed hard with my right arm, dug the toes of my boots into the brickwork and flung my left hand up towards the top of the open window. What exactly happened immediately after that I do not really know. Suddenly there was the sound of breaking glass and I was aware that I was falling forwards. I hit something hard with my ribs and there was a sound of smashing wood as I landed on top of a chair. I then rolled two or three times and came to a stop with my legs jammed under a chest of drawers, completely entangled and wrapped in the curtains. For a few moments I lay there, dazed and winded, unable to move. Then I struggled to free myself from the material, but the more I struggled, the tighter my bonds seemed to become. Finally I realised that it was a curtain which was still attached by one end to the rail and I was rolling myself up into it. By rolling the other way I was able to get free.

Bang, bang, bang! The noise of someone pounding on the door of the room reached my ears. "Are you all right, officer?" shouted a man's voice.

"Yes, yes, hold on a second," I shouted as I slowly staggered to my feet. I glanced quickly around the room. It was obviously a man's room, with everything laid out neat and tidy except for the broken glass, smashed chair and torn curtains. But there was nobody in the room. I quickly looked under the bed and in the wardrobe but there was nothing there at all. Then I suddenly realised that it was a man's voice that had enquired if I was all right. "What the hell's going on?" I shouted, making my way to the door. "There's no key in the lock this side. Open the door," I shouted even louder.

"Listen carefully. She locks the door from the outside and then pushes the key under the door with a piece of wood. It usually goes under the carpet. See if you can find it," said the man's voice.

I hurriedly turned back the carpet in front of the door and sure enough, there was the key. Taking hold of it, I quickly unlocked the door and opened it. There stood a man smartly dressed in a blue pin-striped suit. Sitting on the top of the stairs was Nellie, quietly sobbing into a handkerchief.

"Are you sure you're all right, officer? Let me have a look at you. I'm Dr Browne. I was driving past when I saw you do your dive through the window." Whilst he made a quick examination of me, he told me the following story. "Four months ago, it was the milk-man who scaled the wall outside the window. Three weeks ago, it was an insurance man. Mind you, they managed to do it without breaking anything. Mrs Bradshaw is my patient and, as you know, she's a war widow. After the war she decided to take in lodgers to help pay her way. George Phipps was the one who had this room. Slowly they all left except for George. Then one night he decided to finish it all in this room and took an overdose. Ever since then, she has been a very lonely woman. At first she used to get tradesmen to call to measure up rooms for new carpets, decorating, plumbing – anything, in fact, to get people to come and talk to her. Slowly they all got to know her and refused to come any more. Then about a year ago a man just up the road died suddenly and she saw all the people dealing with it and she decided that this was another way of getting people to be with her and to talk to her. How she devised the complicated plan she used on you all, heaven knows. I think now I will have to make arrangements for her to go to hospital for psychiatric treatment. At least there, she will have someone to talk to."We escorted Nellie Bradshaw, still sobbing, downstairs and I made a cup of tea. From there on, Dusty's advice was never far from my mind and I always found the time to talk to people as I walked the streets of Ryford. You do not have to live in the wilds of the countryside to be lonely: there are more lonely people in one block of flats than in a whole village.

Chapter 4

"Parade! Parade! Attention!" ordered the Section Sergeant, Tom Price. "Night duty relief all present, correct, briefed and ready for your inspection, sir," he continued.

"Thank you, Sergeant. Relief, produce your appointments," ordered Inspector Frank Hillier in his usual officious voice as he marched into the parade room.

This order produced the usual rattling sound as each officer drew his truncheon from his right-hand trouser pocket and held it upright at chest level in front of him. With his left hand he withdrew his whistle from the left-hand breast pocket of his tunic and passed it across to the right hand so that it dangled on its chain through the fingers. The left hand then withdrew and held up the leather wallet containing one pocket-book, three personal injury accident report books (known to all from the Commissioner down as "yellow perils"), three damage-only accident report books, three traffic process books and a pad of forms, which were issued to motorists, for the production at a police station of motor vehicle documents. Lastly, each officer took out a small tin of "marking" materials which consisted of a supply of black cotton, pins, chalk, etc, all used by him to mark particularly vulnerable premises on his beat when he first visited them on his tour of duty. He could then see at a glance if anyone had been near the premises since he was last there.

Inspector Hillier marched along the line, stopped in front of me and ordered, "Let me check the number of books you have in your wallet, Kenyon."

I passed over the wallet and waited for any complaint from the

Duty Officer. The wallet was returned to me with nothing more than a grunt, and Inspector Hillier continued along the line to the end. "Replace appointments," he ordered without turning round and, when the rattling had finished, "Right turn, quick march, to your beats."

I hated the parades before each tour of duty, all the regimentation and bull which, according to the powers that ran the police force, instilled discipline. Their thinking was still in the nineteenth century. Still, things were improving, even during my short amount of service. No longer did the Section Sergeant march us off parade and out along the street in crocodile formation, each officer peeling off as he reached the edge of his beat. Also, just as I had joined, the tunics with clips right up to the neck had been done away with except for ceremonial use. They now had open-neck jackets with breast pockets and shirts with collar and tie. Old habits die hard and these jackets were always referred to as tunics for years after the actual tunics had been withdrawn.

I also detested Inspector Frank Hillier. It was guaranteed that if I was going to get into trouble, Inspector Hillier would be involved in some way. Mind you, I often thought that he might have been a b---, but at least he was a fair b---. He had twenty years service in the police force, having joined in the 1930s and passed his exams for promotion to Sergeant before war was declared. Just before Christmas 1939 he was called up, was given a commission and served in the Household Cavalry until his demobilisation in January 1946. He immediately returned to the police and tried to join the mounted branch. For reasons best known to the senior officers of the force, he never managed it in spite of repeated applications. This had embittered him and as a result he had slowly become more and more officious. His attitude and constant references to his army days soon earned him the nickname of "General Custer".

"Hey, Dick! Are you on seven beat?" called a voice from the reserve and communications room window.

"Yes, that's right. What you got? Something interesting?"

"Not really, just a bail enquiry for Manchester City Force. There's a copy of the message. Call and see if they know chummy and if they are willing to stand surety for him. If they are, ask them to call at the station to sign the necessary forms. Remember to tell them we offer a twenty-four-hour service." The message slip floated gently down into the yard from the window. I bent to pick it up and, as I did so, noticed that I had different-coloured socks on. Good job

General Custer didn't notice them, otherwise I would have received a right telling-off.

I didn't mind doing messages, even the sad ones; I felt it was part of the job and quite an interesting part. At least it was something definite to do, rather than just wandering about and waiting for something to happen. By the time I had walked all the way out to the address it was 11.20 pm, and when I reached the gate I noticed that there were no lights on in the house. I made my way up the path, shone my torch on the front door, located the bell-push and pressed hard. Not a sound did I hear, but just as I had made up my mind that I had better knock, a landing light came on. I heard rustling noises in the hallway, the door opened very slightly and a sexy, husky voice said, "Yes. who is it? What do you want?"

"It's the police. I have a message for Keith Kendle. Is he in?" I said. At the same time I thought to myself, Watch it Dick! With a voice like that she's got plenty of men friends and sounds as if she could be a bit of trouble if you're not careful.

Whilst I was taking a step backwards, the door was opened wide and there in the hallway stood Keith Kendle, complete with a woman's wig and full-length, silk pyjamas and housecoat in the Chinese style. "I'm he, what is it all about?" Never have I delivered a message so fast or been so pleased to get away from an address!

I made my way to the police box and telephoned in that the message had been delivered. I also added what I thought of the reserve man who, it was quite obvious, knew of Keith Kendle but had not warned me. As I left the box I noticed Bill Evans just approaching the box to make his scheduled "ring in". "Hang on, Dick," he said. "I'll give you a walk when I've made my ring."

As we walked together along the boundary road between our two beats, I told my story, much to Bill's amusement – it was the sort of thing that would appeal to his sense of humour which enjoyed seeing a colleague making a fool of himself. "Oh, old KK is well known to be as queer as a nine-bob note," he told me. "He's always being asked to stand surety for one of his old "friends" when they get into trouble."

We chatted on until I mentioned that General Custer had not noticed my odd socks. "Old Custer doesn't see anything below waist level when he inspects a parade. Some say that when he was a Station Sergeant over on "R" division, one PC paraded in brown shoes and got away with it," said Bill.

"Do you know, he has a thing about the number of books I have in my wallet? He checks them at least twice a week," I replied.

"I'm willing to bet you half a crown that you could wear carpet slippers and pyjama trousers on parade for night duty and, providing they were in dark colours, he wouldn't notice," offered Bill.

"Half a crown?", I scoffed, "I would only consider it for a fiver."

By the time booking-off time came, Bill Evans had received pledges from the whole relief for £4 12s 0d, if I would dare to do it. "No way! Nothing less than a fiver," I repeated, knowing full well that nobody else on the relief could afford to make it up to the five pounds.

A challenge like this could not be missed, so Bill came in early for parade that evening. By the time I arrived, the total, with the help of the late turn relief, the civilian telephonist and the night duty Section Sergeant, who must be in on the thing if it was to succeed, had reached £7 2s 6d – more than a week's wages. There was no way out; I had been hoist with my own petard and all that was left to do was to make the necessary arrangements. It was decided that the parade on which the dirty deed would be performed would be in two nights time, Saturday.

Thursday and Friday nights for me were taken up with planning how to get out of it without losing face. Go sick? Annual leave? Time off? Compassionate leave? Commit suicide? They were all possibilities, but with the exception of the last, they were all only delaying tactics. I found the darkest blue pyjama trousers I possessed and borrowed a pair of black imitation leather slip-on slippers. All I could do now was to wait for 9.45 p.m. on Saturday evening. Oh, how I wished I had kept my big mouth shut!

"On parade!" came the order from Section Sergeant Tom Price. "Now then lads, Kenyon had better be right and win this bet, otherwise I'm going to get it in the neck for not spotting him. Therefore, you will all behave as normal and any one of you who thinks of dropping him in it, Evans, had better think again. Yorke, you go and change your helmet to a day duty one so that he has something to moan about." In those days, a night duty helmet was one fitted with a black front badge and top rose so that it did not reflect lights, whereas the day duty one was bright chrome.

A spontaneous quiet ripple of clapping greeted me as I slipped into the parade room. I looked up and down and selected to stand third in line from the door where "General Custer" would enter. Tony Yorke, complete with daytime helmet, stood at number two and the other six men on the relief completed the line.

The Section Sergeant read out all the normal briefings, but somehow I just did not seem to be concentrating on him. That is, until I was snapped out of my own private hell by Tom Price ordering, "Parade! Parade! Attention!" in his normal loud voice and adding in a low one, "The best of luck, you bloody fool." Then he continued, "Night duty relief all present, correct, briefed and ready for your inspection, sir."

"Thank you, Sergeant. Relief, produce your appointments," came the order as Inspector Frank Hillier entered the parade room. I could hardly stop myself from shaking and as it was, I nearly dropped my document wallet. Sweat was pouring off me.

"What do you think you are doing, coming on parade like this? Why didn't you notice him, Sergeant?"

The blood drained from my face, and I was conscious of several heads turned in my direction. I wished the floor would open and swallow me up. I found myself wondering how I could join the Foreign Legion. My mind was a blank.

Then suddenly I became aware of the words, which were being spat out in the familiar manner: "Do you want every criminal in a five-mile radius to see you coming? The taxpayer pays extra so that you can be equipped with the best and you can't be bothered to wear it. What have you got to say for yourself, eh?"

"Very sorry, sir, put the wrong one on by mistake. I do have both here, sir," murmured Tony Yorke.

"Don't let me catch you making the same mistake again. Make sure you change it before you leave the station. Understand?"

"Yes sir. Sorry, sir."

The discovery of such a heinous crime was quite enough for Custer, who continued to the end of the line without even stopping. "Replace your appointments, right turn, quick march, to your beats," came his order, as usual without even turning round.

I obeyed as if in a dream and found myself being borne along with the men on the relief congratulating me. A quiet cheer came from the late relief who, to a man, had waited to see the outcome. By the time I paraded for night duty on Sunday night, I was £7 2s 6d the richer.

I reached the police box on my beat to make my first "ring in", picked up the telephone receiver and reported all correct. The civilian telephonist said, "Hold on, Dick, Inspector Hillier wants a word with you, hold on." Click, buzz, click. "Hillier here."

"PC Kenyon, sir."

"Ah, yes. On the front office counter is the Widows' and Orphans' box. It is completely empty at the moment. I do so hope that it has quite a large sum in it when I check it before going off duty. Understand?"

"Yes, sir," I muttered.

"Not all cavalry officers wear blinkers you know, Kenyon." And so saying he put down the telephone.

"What you got for grub tonight then, Dick?"

I pulled at the draw-string of my small, blue cloth grub-bag and peered inside. "It looks like cheese and tomato. I suppose you've got something revolting and want me to swap with you," I replied.

"Not so. I've got ham. I'll swap you one for one."

"Right, hold on whilst I make the tea."

This conversation, or one similar, was repeated at every police station every night in those days. The Metropolitan police catering service has grown out of all recognition over the years into the dedicated twenty-four-hour service that it operates at most stations today. In addition, the vast mobile and temporary catering facilities needed for such occasions as the Trooping of the Colour, demonstrations, the Derby and the like are a far cry from what was available to us thirty years or so ago. In those days about the only canteens open during the night were those at section houses. This meant that officers had to fetch their own food to cook at night or to bring in sandwiches as the majority did. Somewhere, lost in the history of the

police force, someone had devised a draw-string bag for carrying your grub in. This measured approximately twelve inches by twelve inches and could be hooked onto a button under your tunic or some other place where it could not be seen. It was, of course, not unknown for officers to leave their grub at home, so they had to buy food from the rear of the local coffee bar before it shut. The trouble was, the food had to be hidden away somewhere to get it into the nick without being seen.

Many ingenious methods were devised, but by far the best was the split bamboo raft system. This consisted of a small raft of interlaced split bamboo which fitted exactly into the two breathe-holes on either side of the helmet and created a platform on which to rest a packet of sandwiches. This was also the most popular way of conveying fish and chips to the rear of a convenient set of shops to eat before going into the station. On very cold nights it was not unknown for a policeman to have steam coming from the breathe-holes in the top of the helmet. On other occasions, in hot weather, I have seen officers with molten butter running down their faces.

Personally, I loved being posted to five-beat night duty. Whenever I was, I would not fetch any sandwiches with me. All I would bring was a large pat of butter. At grub time I would only have a cup of tea, then it was a slow walk out to arrive at Munday's Bakery just as the first loaves and rolls were taken from the ovens. Master Baker Bob Wright was allowed so many rolls and so on as droppages each night by the owners, but having worked in the trade for twenty-seven years, he hardly had any and was only too happy to let you have some to eat there and then. Even as I write this, the memory of those wonderful smells and tastes come flooding back to me.

Helmets were not the only items of equipment which came in useful for purposes never dreamt of by the authorities who gave them to us. The issue of raincoats in the late 'fifties to replace the capes which all officers rolled and carried with them when rain was forecast was not as popular as might have been expected. The reason was that a cape had a multitude of uses besides protecting its wearer from the rain (which it did very well provided that you held it slightly out and away from you so that the water running down dripped clear of your trousers). These other uses were varied. In its rolled-up form, the cape was a deadly weapon in the hands of an experienced officer. A whack around the legs or ears with one of these delivered as a form of instant justice to a young miscreant was a never-to-be-forgotten experience, as I know to my cost from my

formative years – something which would never be tolerated by today's civil rights, anti-discipline, talk-nicely-to-them-poor-little-darlings society that we live in. In those days, in the vast majority of cases, if a cape recipient told their parents, they got another whacking. I read that today's attitude is what is known as "progress", but I often wonder. When worn, the cape could cover a multitude of sins. For example, it was possible to walk with your hands in your pockets without being detected, marvellous in the cold weather when the regulation-issue woollen gloves failed to do their job which was almost always. Another use was that you could hide shopping underneath it. Personal shopping on duty was a serious offence against the discipline code and it was almost impossible to get your purchases back to the station undetected without the use of the cape.

I stood with my back to the wall of Boots the chemist in Ryford High Street. The time was 4.30 pm and I reckoned that providing there was no Duty Officer or Section Sergeant about, I could get a cup of tea from the back of Woolworths before they closed. I double-checked up and down the High Street. No senior officers in sight, so I eased myself into the alleyway between Boots and Woolworths. One last check and I was gone. On reaching the back of Woolworths, I found my way to the back door barred by hundreds of small rose bushes, all of which were in various stages of dying. Carefully I picked my way through them, tapped on the door, opened it and stepped inside.

" 'Allo then, Dick. Fancy a cuppa?" asked Rose Kettle, the canteen manageress, who always said that with a name like hers it was the only job she could do.

"Yes please, Rose, m'luv. Mind if I smoke?"

"Don't care if you burst into flames, but watch where you put your ash, OK?"

Ten minutes later I thanked Rose and left by the back door. As I did so, I met the shop manager who was dumping more rose bushes. "What's all this then?" I enquired.

"I forgot to tell anyone to water them in the shop and they've got to such a state we can't sell them. The dustman can take them away when he comes on Friday."

"What a waste! Some of them look as though they could be saved."

"Well, take your pick and help yourself. You're more than welcome."

Thanking the manager, I selected about ten and put them to one side. My idea was that I could fetch my cape out with me after grub and just before it was time to book off, collect the bushes, hide them under my cape and smuggle them into the station cycle-shed without them even being seen. I could leave them there, book off and then cycle home with them under my cape.

All went well with the plan until I was about a hundred yards from the station. It was then that Inspector Frank Hillier walked out of the station yard and turned left so that he was walking directly towards me. There was nowhere to escape to. I could do nothing but carry on walking and hope that the Inspector didn't notice. To the best of my knowledge there has never been a blind serving Inspector in any police force. It was blind he was going to have to be if he was not to notice that I looked like a full-term mother-to-be of quads. "All correct, sir," I said as I drew level with "General Custer" at the same time giving a smart eyes-right; you did not salute if you were wearing a cape, you either stood to attention or gave an eyes right or left.

"Thank you, Kenyon, but what have you got under your cape?" he enquired.

My mind raced. How could I get out of this? I had nothing written by the manager of Woolworths to say that I could take the roses, so it would appear that I had stolen them. The consequences of this were only too plain. "Under my cape, sir?" I asked, playing for time and praying that some reasonable excuse would conjure itself out of thin air.

"Yes, man, under your cape."

"Ten rose bushes, sir," I replied, hoping that this would satisfy him. After all, it was the truth as far as it went.

"Well, what are you doing with them?"

Suddenly the answer hit me. It was so simple that it could not fail. "Property found abandoned, sir, believed stolen, sir," I answered. This meant that I lost my rose bushes but it also meant that I would avoid any more serious consequences.

"Oh, I see," said the Inspector. "Make out a full report about them, then. On your way."

"Yes, sir, thank you, sir." So saying, I continued on to the station.

When I paraded for late turn next day, there was a message for me to see Inspector Hillier before I left the station. Immediately after the parade I reported to his office, very apprehensive. "Ah, Kenyon. The owner of the roses has been traced. He does not want them back and asked us to dispose of them for him. I thought it would be rather nice if they were planted in the garden in front of the station. Maybe you could find time during your refreshment period to do the job for me, if you take my point."

"Yes, sir, very good, sir, no problem at all, sir," I stammered as I backed out of his office. Those same roses are still in the garden in front of Kyford nick.

Only once did I have "General Custer" at a real disadvantage, and that was by accident. It was the following Fireworks Night, a night that I will remember with pleasure to my dying day. My relief was posted to night duty that week and I was lucky enough, or unlucky enough, depending on your point of view, not to have been selected

to be one of Ryford's contribution to "A" Division to help in the policing of the revellers in Trafalgar Square. I could never really understand why thousands of people found it necessary or, come to that, even enjoyable to gather together on this particular date. New Year's Eve, yes, but why 5th November? Still, it takes all sorts!

My posting that night was to one and two beats. These were the ones that were superimposed over the three High Street patrols.

As usual we were briefed on parade of the latest crime trends on our "patch". I often wondered if the CID and we uniformed police officers were in the same police force. They blamed us for not discovering crimes, and even more for not catching the perpetrators, whereas we always grumbled that unless the criminal walked into the station and gave himself up, they couldn't detect a gas leak with a lighted match. These hostile feelings between the two branches of the force even showed itself in the form of outright contempt by certain CID officers. They had conveniently forgotten that even they had done their time in the uniform branch. The rivalry between us always meant that we were ever hopeful that we would capture a major criminal in the process of committing his crime. However the most likely "excitement" that night would be when the pubs turned out. Normally these were comparatively quiet and orderly, with just the occasional patron, slightly worse for wear, singing his way home. Ryford did not have a drunk problem.

"Officer, officer, come quick. There's a drunk offering to fight anyone. He's outside the Duke's Head," gasped a small, dapper man who had come running around the corner and almost knocked into me. I resisted the temptation of saying that if everyone left him alone he would more than likely go home with no trouble. Somehow the public did not seem to be able to accept this perfectly sound method of policing. Assuring the man that I would deal with the matter, I slowly made my way around the corner and into North Street.

Although I had only a limited amount of service, I had already learnt a very important lesson about two months earlier. On that occasion, I had been walking to my patrol on the High Street with my mentor "Dusty" Miller. As we neared the Greyhound pub, three large navvies spilled out onto the pub forecourt, fighting for all they were worth. Actually, one always claimed that he was trying to stop the other two by punching the pair of them. Immediately I saw them I had eagerly said to Dusty, "Come on, let's arrest them." I was just about to hurry towards them when Dusty's hand grabbed my shoulder and pulled me into a shop doorway. "Whoa down, youngster, hold on a minute. What's the point of diving in on them now and getting all three turned on us. Wait and watch. It won't take long before they have punched themselves out, then we can walk in and pick up the pieces." About three minutes later, one of the contestants was sitting on the ground holding a bleeding nose, whilst the other two had their arms wound around one another, just about managing to stand up. "Now we can have three arrests with no trouble. Always remember that!" So saying, Dusty stepped out of the doorway and made his slow and sedate way towards the three men.

Tonight was different though. As I turned the corner I saw PC Tony Yorke struggling with a comparatively small man who was continuously shouting, "Oi'll bloody murder yer, the lots of yers." I quickened my pace to a trot to go to Tony's assistance.

"I've phoned the nick for the van," said a bus inspector as I passed him.

"Thanks," I said. "Right, Tony, the van's on its way, let's get him." So saying, I joined the mêlée. After what seemed an eternity but in actual fact was only about five minutes, during which time Tony and I were fighting a losing battle with one fighting-drunk Irishman, the van arrived on the scene. With the aid of the van

driver, Ernie "Blossom" Trevellyn, and the Section Sergeant, Tom Price, we managed to get the drunk into the van and to the nick. In spite of the combined might of the three of us in the van, our prisoner continued fighting.

Once we reached the station, we managed to get the drunk out of the van and spreadeagled on the ground in the station yard with one of us holding grimly to a limb each. "Right, lads," came the voice of Tom Price. "On the count of three, all lift together. One, two, threeee – bloody hell, I've pulled his bleedin' leg orf!"

If it wasn't for the fact that the loss of the leg from just below the knee apparently made no difference at all to the fighting capabilities of Paddy, I have no doubt the remainder of us would have been rolling around laughing. As it was, the loss of this artificial encumbrance appeared to be the signal for Paddy to really start fighting according to what he was shouting. What he had been doing for the past ten minutes or so, we really did not know, but he assured us that he was being "gentle wivs yer all uptus now." So saying, he turned into a raging tornado on one and a half legs. He managed to get one arm free from Tony Yorke and promptly punched me in the left ear, causing me to lose grip of the other arm. "Blossom" Trevellyn held on grimly to the complete leg. Tom Price flung the wooden leg across the yard and rushed forward to grab hold of the flailing stump. As he did so, Paddy twisted left and right and slammed the stump in the general direction of the fast-advancing Tom Price. It was then that Tom achieved his life-long ambition of being eligible to audition for the position of soprano soloist with the Metropolitan Police Male Voice Choir. Holding his nether regions, he slumped to his knees, tears streaming down his face, and took no further part in the proceedings.

"What is happening here?" came the officious question from the Duty Officer, Inspector "General Custer" Hillier as he stood on the steps which led from the yard up into the charge-room.

"What the hell do you think is happening, you daft twot," I heard the voice of Tony Yorke whisper from behind clenched teeth as he tried vainly to recover hold of his part of Paddy's anatomy.

"Watch out there, you three, he's going to get away. I'll stop him myself, you incompetent fools." So saying, "General Custer" launched himself down the steps at Paddy. What he didn't know was that Blossom had managed to get onto his knees, still holding onto the complete leg. This gave him the opportunity to apply the necessary purchase to the limb to pull it out from under Paddy. At the same time I was coming up from the ground with a clenched fist aiming a punch with all my might at the upper half of Paddy. Blossom heaved; Paddy fell forward; my punch missed completely and continued upwards; "General Custer" came through the air towards where Paddy should have been. Then, suddenly, there was dreadful pain shooting up and down my right arm and my hand felt as if every bone in it had been broken. Paddy crashed to the ground with "General Custer" landing on top of him, out cold.

Seizing the opportunity, Blossom and Tony dragged the Inspector aside and carried the now exhausted Paddy into the charge-room. Tom Price made his way painfully up the steps, looking for all the world like a rotund, bow-legged ballerina trying to walk on points with a rugby ball between her legs, at the same time calling out for the reserve man to telephone for the Divisional Surgeon; "General Custer" came back into the world of the living, holding the right side of his face and screaming to be let loose at that drunken Irish swine who had punched him. I helped him to his feet and up the stairs into the station, keeping my right hand well out of sight. As soon as I had deposited him in the front office, I rushed to the toilets and placed my rapidly swelling right hand under a running cold tap.

Did I say I had Frank Hillier at a disadvantage? Not for long. Parade book entries for Friday 29th November: "Metropolitan Police Athletic Association. The following officers are warned to attend Blackheath Road Section House gymnasium on Wednesday 11th December at 7.30 pm for training for the MPAA Boxing Tournament – PCs Yorke, Trevellyn and Kenyon. Signed: Inspector Hillier."

If Inspector Hillier did things by the book, other, more senior officers took a more unorthodox approach. I had been attached to station office duties and on the first day was posted early turn. I duly reported to the Station Officer at 5. 45 am. All went well until about 11 am, when the Station Officer said, "Keep an eye on things whilst I go for a you-know-what" and off he went to the toilets. I was sitting in the chair behind the big desk reading the Occurrence Book, the book in which everything that happens on Ryford's manor and is reported to the police is recorded.

Suddenly, the door which the public use crashed open and through it bustled a tall, balding, red-faced man of about fifty, wearing an unkempt suit which looked as if it had been slept in. Without a word, he lifted up the flap at the end of the counter, unbolted the gate and strode into the front office.

"Just a minute, you can't come in here," I protested, jumping up and moving towards the intruder. Without saying a word, he swept me aside with one arm and planted himself down in the chair I had just vacated. "Listen, either you get out of here very fast or you'll find yourself nicked," I said in a loud and irritated voice.

"Fetch me the books," ordered the man in the chair.

"Listen to me, mate, and listen good. I'll give you ten seconds to get out of that bleeding chair and on the other side of the counter or you'll be sitting in the bloody charge-room. Understand?"

"Nicely and explicitly put, young man. Now do as you're told and get me the books." So saying, the man took a fountain pen from his breast pocket.

"That's it, mate, that's your lot," I said, taking a step towards the intruder.

"I'm Radler, Mad Dave Radler, the District Commander. You may have heard of me. Now get me the books," he replied imperturbably, scribbling an illegible mark underneath the last entry in the Occurrence Book in bright green ink.

Little warning bells rang in my head. I had heard about Mad Dave Radler and some of the stories I had heard were vaguely the same as I was involved in now. "If you're who you say you are, sir, may I see your silver token," I asked in a very polite, servile voice. All police officers at Commander and above carried a silver token by which to identify themselves; we lesser mortals had a printed cardboard warrant card.

The man sighed and said in a very loud voice which verged on shouting, "Do as you are told and get me the books."

"This is the last time of asking. Either show me your silver token or you're nicked, sir," I told him in an exasperated voice.

Slowly the man put his hand into his inside pocket and drew from it a silver token. He carefully laid it on the Occurrence Book facing me and was just about to say something when the door from the charge-room opened and the returning Station Officer said, "All correct, sir. Get the books out for Mr Radler to see then, lad." Never had the books been taken ou from the filing cupboard, opened and placed in front of the District Commander as fast as they were that morning. I was trying to behave if I was very busy and to keep as much in the background as possible, but when he had finished and was about to leave he called me over to him. "At least you remembered to ask me for my token in the end. This is the first station I've been to this month where I've not been arrested." He

then gave me and the Station Officer a lecture on the proper security of a police station.

"Now you know part of the reason he's known as Mad Dave Radler," said the Station Officer after our District Commander had left.

Apart from "Mad Dave's" occasional whirlwind visits, the most senior officer to come into our everyday lives was Superintendent Banford. It was he who called me into his office one day after I had almost completed the first of my two years as a probationer.

"Ah, there you are, Kenyon. Come in", he said, looking over the top of his spectacles at me from behind his desk. I marched briskly forward into the office and came to a halt immediately in front of the desk. Turning to his clerk who was standing beside him, the Superintendent asked, "Is this the file, Smythe?"

"Yes, sir," replied Don Smythe, passing over a comparatively thick file on the front of which I just glimpsed my name and warrant number.

"Right, you can leave us. Close the door."

"Sir," said the clerk as he left the office, closing the door behind him.

"Right then, lad, what's all this about then?"

"Begging your pardon, sir," I replied, "what's what about?"

"This application to become a dog-handler. Surely you know you can't specialise until you have finished your probation of two years?"

"Yes sir."

"Why submit it then?"

"I thought that I should make my ambition plain, sir. I thought that if I didn't apply, you wouldn't know just how much I wanted to specialise in dog- handling. It's why I joined the police, sir." I blurted all this out before I realised that I had not intended to bare my soul in this way. It was true I had joined the police to become a dog-handler. It was also a fact, although he didn't know it, that his clerk, Don Smythe, who was well aware of my yearning, had tipped me off a few days earlier that Ryford's dog-handler had volunteered to go to Cyprus with his dog. This would mean that a vacancy would occur for handling duties very soon.

"As and when a vacancy occurs, I will put an entry in the parade book, calling for volunteers. You can apply then, understand?"

"Yes, sir, sorry sir," I replied.

"Don't sorry me, lad. He who doesn't ask doesn't get. Right, dismissed."

"Yes, sir, thank you, sir," I said, about-turned and marched out of the office. Superintendent Banford had been kind and I felt that I had done myself no harm by letting him know of my ambition to be a dog-handler. That ambition was as strong as ever and I was prepared to let as many senior officers as possible know how desperately I wanted to achieve my goal.

CHAPTER 5

I made the tea, poured it and sat down at the table. "Fancy a game of crib?" I asked.

"Sure, where's the board?"

Being early grub-time did have its advantages, one of which was that you could get to a pack of cards and crib-board before the others got in. We were just nearing the end of the first game when the canteen door burst open and two more of the relief came in.

"After the easy way we keep ambushing you, you should have arrow wounds all over you," gloated Bill Evans, the chief of the Blue Bottle Indians.

"Just you wait, I'll get my own back," I retorted. As I went down the stairs to the front office to book out, I realised that tonight was the perfect one for wreaking my revenge on Bill Evans and his tribe – they were now over-confident, so would be off-guard. On the way out I went to my locker and took from it my "weapon" which I had placed there several days ago, waiting for the right moment. I checked that it was primed and loaded, slipped it carefully into my trouser-belt and left the station to return to my High Street patrol.

A few weeks previously it had been my son's birthday and our only wealthy relative had sent a present of a replica Peacemaker six-shot revolver. The fact that he was only one year old had not influenced the choice of present in the slightest. Unlike most toy guns, this was made as an authentic replica with rotating chambers and extractable bullets; each bullet had a brass cap which could be removed and loaded with exploding caps. When fired, the revolver gave a loud bang and the chambers revolved, giving the impression that it was real.

By 2 am I was positioned in the only shop doorway which was deep enough for me to lay an ambush from without any risk of being seen. When I arrived at the shop I was dismayed to discover that the window display had been altered since the previous day and that now all vision along the High Street was blocked. However, I was resolved to carry out my plan. I settled back and lit a cigarette. There would be ample time to finish it before my chosen victim, the Indian Chief, was due out of the station and passed by on his way to his patrol area. At 2.35 am I heard the footsteps on the pavement . The usual measured steps, slowly making their way towards me. Every now and then they would stop and there was a pause as their maker window-shopped. I eased the revolver from its hiding place and tensed as the footsteps came nearer and nearer. As I was unable to see my victim, my timing must be absolutely right. Too early and the Indian Chief would be able to dive for cover into another doorway. Too late and the visual effect of the revolver would be lost.

Now! No, wait! The footsteps had stopped. After what seemed like an eternity they started again. NOW! I leapt out, crouching low, firing as I came. Bang, bang, bang, bang, bang, bang – six loud reports echoed along the shops. Sleeping pigeons in their ledges fluttered into wakefulness; a roaming tomcat rushed for cover across the road; and the victim slumped to the ground, clutching his chest and making strange gurgling sounds.

As I launched myself into action I was chanting "Revenge is sweet" "Another Indian bites the dust". However, I now stood on the pavement in full uniform, mouth gaping open and smoking revolver in my hand. There, instead of a 28-year-old uniformed Indian Chief with a feather in his helmet badge denoting his designation for the night, there lay a late-middle-aged man dressed in civilian clothes.

In spite of my shock I reacted quickly. I turned and ran off down a side street. Swiftly I climbed over the fences at the rear of the shops and emerged back into the High Street about seventy yards above the ambush position. I then ran to the crumpled form on the pavement. "What has happened to you, sir? Are you injured?" I asked in best training-school tradition.

Bending low, I was just able to hear the faint murmur, "A policeman did it, I've been shot by a policeman."

"A policeman?" I said in an incredulous voice. "That's impossi-

ble." I carried out a swift examination of my victim and said, "You lie there and I'll call an ambulance."

At the hospital the casualty officer asked what the victim had said when I found him. "Something which sounded like he had been shot by a policeman," I replied.

"Strange," said the doctor, "that's what he keeps on repeating here. I can find nothing physically wrong with him. I'll have to keep him in for observation and psychiatric examination."

I breathed a sigh of relief that there were no signs of heart attack brought on by shock and off I went to question the victim.

"I work on the print in London. I caught the last train to Ryford and was walking home through the High Street when a policeman in full uniform jumped out of a shop doorway and fired a gun at me," said Jonathan Charles Hardy, aged fifty-nine as he lay on the hospital bed.

"Thank you," I said in a quiet, reassuring voice. "You rest now and I will go to your house and inform your wife so that she does not worry about you. Then she will be able to come and visit you." With this I rose to leave, but as I did so, I felt my foot touch something which went skidding across the polished floor of the men's medical ward.

Leaving the ward, I hurried along the corridor. The sooner I was away from the hospital and able to write up my report the better, I thought. Suddenly I heard the clatter of a nurse's footsteps hurrying along behind me. Without a word, the nurse, who had a very strange expression on her face, caught up with me, pressed a replica Peacemaker toy revolver into my hand and returned the way she had come.

Report completed, I booked off duty and went to the locker-room. There on my locker was a sign which read:

WE WILL REVENGE THE MAKER OF MARKS ON WHITE PARCHMENT.

Signed: he who wears the strange hat, Chief of the Blue Bottle Indians.

Bill Evans was becoming a real menace with his warped sense of humour and practical jokes. I was his victim often enough, but nothing like his favourite target, PC Tony Yorke. Towards the end of one particular night duty, Tony made a discovery whilst posted to the High Street. Every morning at about 5.30 am, a milk lorry pulled up outside Lyons Corner House and exchanged two full milk churns for two empty ones which were left in the doorway every night. These churns made an excellent seat – a bit cold, but a seat which could be used to take the weight off one's aching feet. The doorway was not very deep and anyone sitting in it could easily be seen from the road, but if you wore your cape you could sit with the cape covering the churn. Done properly, you looked just like a small policeman. These churns had been used for years by policemen but like so many things, a young probationer had to find this out for himself.

Tony eased himself onto the churn, gave a sigh of relief and arranged his cape neatly around himself. It was not long before he dozed off. It was his bad luck that Bill Evans happened to cycle past on the way to his beat after grub and noticed him. The temptation was just too much for Bill when he saw the hunched figure of Tony sitting on the churn asleep. The opportunity was just too good to be true, especially to someone with a warped mind like Bill's.

In a flash Bill knew what he was going to do. He stood on the pedals of his cycle and got up speed quickly. As fast as his legs would go, he pedalled off up the High Street to the wrought-iron gates which guarded the entrance to the park. As he reached the gates, he jumped off, leant his cycle against one of the pillars and climbed up and over and dropped into the park. He ran down the path, around the corner to the gardener's shed. Here he searched until he found all the items he needed to make his idea work. He rushed back to the gate, pushed the items through it and climbed over. Gathering the bits and pieces together, he cycled as fast as he could back towards Lyons Corner House.

Quietly he pulled up about thirty yards short of the shop. Propping the cycle against the kerb, he went into a deep doorway to construct the apparatus. About five minutes later he crept stealthily towards Lyons Corner House. As he got closer he could hear Tony's steady breathing. There could be no doubt that he was asleep. Eventually Bill reached the doorway and took a deep breath as he gently slid the stem of a white chrysanthemum behind the front plate of Tony's helmet. Next, he carefully lifted the front of the cape and folded it as best he could into Tony's lap, then slid a six-foot-long garden cane between Tony's arms and his body, resting the bottom end firmly under the ledge of the doorway. He then slipped a bucket in front of Tony and from it pulled a piece of string. On the end of the string was a bent nail which was hooked through the eyehole of an old boot. He adjusted the length of string so that the boot rested on the top of the bucket and tied the other end to the top of the cane. His work completed, he crept backwards across the road and surveyed his handiwork. He was beside himself with glee at the overall impression.

It was all too good for Bill alone; he just had to share it with someone else. Swiftly he crossed the road to his cycle and rode off to the nearest telephone box. From there he put up a call to the information room at New Scotland Yard for the local wireless car to meet him at that location re information. It was also to approach from the railway station end of the High Street. Within three minutes the car arrived and Bill told them what he had done. Slowly the car drove past Lyons Corner House in both directions with the crew doubled up with laughter. By the end of the tour of duty, the whole relief knew about the episode and pulled Tony's leg unmercifully.

The next night, Tony took great care not to sit down anywhere. At about 4.30 am he was standing in the doorway of W H Smith's the newsagents when the lorry delivering the bundles of newspapers and magazines arrived. "Morning. Not bad this morning, is it?" greeted the driver.

"No, not bad at all."

"Here you are then, here's your paper." So saying, the driver handed down a newspaper to Tony. This was one of the perks of night duty if the right driver was on.

"Many thanks."

"OK, me old cock, see yer tomorrow," said the driver as he drove off.

Tony glanced at the headlines and idly opened the pages. It was then that he saw it. Dead centre of page three. A photograph of a crouching policeman with a chrysanthemum in his helmet, fishing an old boot out of a bucket with a cane and a piece of string. The caption read, "PC G Nome. It is his vigilance which allows us to sleep safely in our beds at night."

Luckily the photograph had been taken so that it was impossible to read the officer's number or to identify the location, but it was obvious that Tony had been spotted by someone with a camera before he had woken up. For months this photograph hung in place of honour in the canteen at Ryford nick. And Tony Yorke took an oath of undying vengeance on Bill Evans.

CHAPTER 6

"'Er,officer, I wants to report something really bad."

"Hallo, Nellie. What's it this time, a peeping Tom or a lost pussy?" I sighed. Nellie Bradshaw had been released from hospital after treatment following the episode of the non-existent lodger, but it was always me she seemed to find when she was on one of her wandering sprees.

"Neither of them, so there," she snapped at me. "If you're going to be like that, I won't tell yer, will I?"

"Now, now, Nellie, don't get upset. You know I'll help you if I can, don't you?"

"Yeah, that's true. At least you try. Most of them tell me to clear orf."

"OK, Nellie, what is so bad that you want to report to me?" I asked.

"Well, it's like this 'ere, innit. I has me supper, and I'm taking me clothes orf when this peeper taps on me winder, don't he? So I tells him to clear off, but he takes no notice and just stands there with 'is nose pressed to the glass. So I thinks to meself, if I gets dressed again, 'e'll go away. So I starts putting me dress back on...."

"Hang on! Hang on! I thought you had something to tell me that was real bad," I interrupted.

"I'm telling yer, ain't I? Don't rush me. It's not right, it's not."

"What's not right?" I sighed.

"If you clears your lugs out and let me get on with it, yer'll find out, won't yer?"

"All right, Nellie, tell me your own way."

"Well, as I was saying, I puts me dress back on and thinks to meself that I could do with another cuppa, so I puts on the kettle, then my Timmy wants to go out so I opens the door and out 'e goes. I makes me tea, opens the door and calls 'im, don't I?"

"Who, the peeper or your Timmy?" I asked flippantly.

"My Timmy of course, yer daft sod. Timmy, Timmy, Timmy I calls but he doesn't come, so I puts on me coat and goes looking for 'im. After about 'arf an 'our searching, that's when I finds 'im, don't I?"

"Well, if you've found the cat, then all's well that ends well," I said, turning to leave.

"No, it ain't my Timmy, its 'im, the poor little bleeder. They deserve to be horse-whipped whoever they are, don't they?" she said in an agitated voice as she grabbed hold of my sleeve.

"Him who?" I asked in an uncertain voice. Somehow I had the feeling that Nellie was serious and that this was something a lot worse than cats and peepers. Slowly I turned back and gently took her shoulders in my hands. It was then that I noticed she had tears in her eyes. "Now, now, come on, Nellie. Tell me what you found or what you saw," I said as gently as I could.

"I'm trying, ain't I, but you keep putting yer oar in, don't yer? I'm looking for my Timmy everywhere. 'E likes to play games and 'ide from me, as yer well know. Well, I gets to the back of number eleven John Street."

"How do you know it's number eleven?" I asked.

"Because it's got the number chalked on the gate, ain't it. I creeps in and opens the coal-'ouse door, just in case Timmy's 'iding in there. That's when I 'ears a funny whimpering sort of noise, so I strikes a match on the wall, and that's when I sees 'im, don't I?"

By this time tears were rolling down her cheeks as the memory of whatever she had seen came rushing back to her. "Take your time, Nellie, take your time," I said as soothingly as possible.

"If I lays me 'ands on them bleeders that done it, I'll swing for 'em," she suddenly screamed.

"Steady, steady, Nellie. Tell me what you saw."

"I strikes me match, don't I, and there in the corner, on top of the coal, is a little kid with a lump of rope round 'is neck. I'll kill the bastards I will. Just let me get me 'ands on 'em, that's all." With that she collapsed on my shoulders in uncontrollable sobbing.

If only half of what she had told me was correct, I was in desperate

need of assistance, including a Woman Police Officer. Not only that but Nellie was now in such a state that she needed medical treatment. Slowly I walked Nellie across the road to the telephone box and telephoned for urgent assistance. I also asked for two ambulances, one to take Nellie to hospital and one to stand by in case it was needed.

The wireless car arrived on the scene about three minutes later, closely followed by the first ambulance. A car-to-car message from the Duty Officer told us to wait until he arrived with a WPC. The Duty Officer led the way down the alleyway to the gate at the rear of number eleven John Street. Sure enough, there was the number chalked on the gate, just as Nellie had described. The Duty Officer, the WPC and I entered the yard together, torches at the ready. On the nod of the Duty Officer, I threw open the coal-shed door and the beams of our three torches illuminated the interior. There, on top of a small pile of coal dust, huddled a child of about three years old. It wore no clothes and was covered in coal dust. There were obviously deep wounds across its back and legs, many of which were still bleeding. Around its neck was tied a length of rope, secured to a ring set high up in the ceiling. If the child moved off the mound of coal dust, it would have strangled itself. It was impossible to tell at that stage what sex it was. As the torch-lights played on the child, it kept screaming, "I didn't do it, I didn't do it." WPC Gloria Brown eased her way into the confined space. "There, there, we're not going to hurt you," she soothed in a quiet and gentle voice. How she managed to gain the confidence of that child in twenty minutes I will never know. Slowly she backed out of the shed with the child wrapped in her top- coat. She walked with it to the waiting ambulance and went off to the hospital.

"Let me go with you, sir," I pleaded with the duty officer. "I want to help nick whoever's responsible for that poor little sod. Just let me get my hands on them."

"No, you don't. I've called the night duty CID and I will go in along with them. We don't want you being done for causing grievous bodily harm, do we?"

"Come on, sir. It was me that got the info. Let me have a go at them," I begged.

"Kenyon," snapped the Duty Officer, "this is an order. You will go to the hospital and see how your informant is now. You will then make the necessary arrangements for her to be conveyed home if they are not going to keep her in. You will also make out a report on

the information you received and the illness in the street of your informant. Understand?"

"Yes sir, but..."

"Kenyon!"

"Sir?"

"On your way!"

"Yes sir."

As I walked slowly away, the words of "Dusty" Miller's lecture to me when I was learning beats came flooding back. "You'll feel the urge to take revenge on behalf of the innocent," he had told me. "Don't do it, because it will always go sour on you and you'll be in the wrong, not them." I realised, now, that I had felt a rage stronger almost than any other emotion I had ever experienced, that Dusty had been teaching me one of the most important lessons a policeman can learn. All the same, there were to be many situations in my police career when it was almost impossible not to take the law into my own hands. I am proud to say that although sorely tempted on many occasions, I did always manage to control myself – just.

Some months later, the boy's father, who had been arrested by the CID that night, was sentenced to several years' imprisonment. I still could not understand why we in the uniformed branch did not have much respect for the abilities of our plain-clothes colleagues in the CID. After all, we all wanted to catch criminals, no matter if it was for lead-stealing from the building site or the more major criminals such as those who were committing a puzzling series of safe-breaking incidents on our own patch in Ryford. So it was with a mixture of apprehension and interest that I looked forward to my attachment to the CID.

Every police constable during his two-year probationary service receives attachment postings to the various specialist departments which together make up the police service. At that time, the attachments were usually for one week and, except for a very few cases, were regarded as an inconvenience by all the officers in the specialist departments. In the mid-1950s, these attachments were confined to those departments readily available in the immediate area. Working on the outskirts of the Metropolitan Police District, as we did on Ryford sub-division, there was no likelihood of our doing attachments to Thames Division or the mounted branch. Our attachments were confined to CID, court, traffic patrol, station office and dog-handling. Most probationers felt that the attachments were a bit of a farce; after all, a tea boy or "gofer" is much the same no matter where you are. This applies to the majority of the time that I spent on attachments except that I did manage on every one to become involved in matters which related to that particular department and which left them firm in the knowledge that I had been there.

My attachment to the CID was, of course, in plain clothes and at the start I worried a great deal as to the type of clothing to wear: should I be formal or informal? Eventually I decided that it would be formal. The only formal outfit that I possessed was my wedding suit, which I could still fit into – it would puzzle me to do so now. So, dressed in white shirt, spotted tie, blue suit and black shoes, I reported to the CID office at 9 am on the first day.

"PC Kenyon reporting for CID attachment, sir." I said to a tall man who was smartly dressed in civilian clothes and was standing in the Detective- Inspector's office by the desk. I did not recognise the man but knew that our old DI had received promotion and that a new DI was to be posted to us. This was he, I assumed.

"There's no need to call me sir, Sergeant will do, lad," said a voice from the direction of the desk.

I blinked and stood there, amazed. There was not the slightest sign of lip movement from the man, yet his voice was as clear as a bell. "Can you get three teas from the canteen? I'll pay you as soon as you get back, OK?" Again, there was no sign of movement on his lips.

"Yes, OK, Sarge, but how do you manage to speak so clearly doing that?" I enquired.

"I always speak this way," said the voice of a bald-headed man, aged about forty, as he raised his head over the level of the desk-top. "Before you do that, see if you can find a small gold earring on the floor over here. I'll be damned if I can see it, and I can't charge chummy here with stealing it if I haven't got it as evidence, can I?" So saying, he indicated the tall man standing by the desk.

My ventriloquist was in fact an expert house-breaker who had been caught during the night in the house of one of our local JPs. Not a particularly auspicious way in which to start my attachment.

I did, however, make up for it later in the week. I was cycling my way home after my tour of duty with the CID when I noticed three youths aged about eighteen or nineteen acting suspiciously on the forecourt of Ryland railway station. By the glimpse I had of them, it appeared that the two taller and older of the group were trying to take something from inside the raincoat of the smaller younger youth, who was apparently struggling. I made a "U" turn on my pedal-cycle and went back to the forecourt. The youths were still struggling. Propping my cycle against the wall of the station, I walked across the cobbles to the three youths.

"I am a police officer. What's going on here then?" I said in my best official voice, at the same time producing my warrant card.

Bang! Slip! Splat! It all happened in a split second. Two of the youths turned and pushed me hard in the chest with their shoulders, I slipped on the wet cobble-stones and ended up flat on my back. As I gathered myself and got up, I could see all three youths running away together up the High Street. Why they didn't split up I've no idea, but they ran in a tight group. I set off after them, slightly winded from the push and fall and from the fact that I smoked too much. It was not long before I was gasping for air. Amazingly, in spite of this, I began to close on the three youths. After about 200 yards I managed to draw alongside them and bustle them into a shop doorway.

With my back against one side of the doorway and my arm outstretched onto the other, I held them in the doorway whilst I heaved and gulped for air. I had no idea that I was in such bad condition. Slowly, as I recovered, I took stock of my captives. All three were in a worse state than I was, if that was possible. They leant on the window and on the door, wheezing, choking and sucking in air as fast as possible but none of them had taken their hands out of their raincoat pockets. This fact had escaped me until now. The more I thought about it, the more I realised they had run with their hands in their raincoat pockets as well. "Right then, you three, what have you got in your pockets?" I asked them when I had got my breath back enough to speak.

"Ain't got nothin', have we?" gasped the youngest of the three, pulling the lining of his pockets out with his hands. The same applied to all of them.

It didn't make sense. Why run with their hands in their pockets if they had nothing in them? "Come here, one of you, let me search you," I ordered.

The eldest stepped forward and held out his arms. "What makes you think we've done anything wrong, then?" he asked, trying to bluff it out.

As soon as I touched his body, I detected his ill-gotten gains. I could hardly miss them: wrapped around his body, extending from just above the top of his thighs to under his armpits and hidden under his shirt, were several layers of sheet lead. All of the youths were the same; there was no wonder they had run with their hands in their pockets, trying to support their weight. The struggling I had witnessed in the station forecourt was them helping each other to hoist their loads into a more comfortable position. They had stolen the lead from the building site at Crystal Palace, where they had been working as labourers.

As one of them said in court the next morning, "If it 'ad been anythin' else but bluey we 'ad with us, the copper wouldn't 'ave seen our arses for dust!" How right he was. If only they had known it, another ten yards that night and they could have walked away from me without me having enough breath to stop them.

Strangely, the anti-uniform feeling by CID officers became worse the higher the rank of officer, some of whom took matters to excess, as happened a few weeks later. I was posted late turn, 2 pm to 10 pm, on the wireless car. It was common practice for each relieving crew to be ready to take over about twenty minutes before the actual time, so at 1.40 pm I was changing into my uniform jacket when Ernie "Blossom" Trevellyn poked his head round the door and enquired if I was ready.

"Just coming," I said. "What's on then, we got a call?"

"That's right, my dear. You get your skates on and I'll make sure Blossom's harness and fodder are OK and then we'll be on our way," said Ernie as he left to go and check that the car had plenty of oil, fuel and water, that all the tyres were of the correct pressure and that there was no unreported damage. He then booked the car out in his name and we had officially taken over. I, in turn, checked with the early-turn operator as to any local lost or stolen motor vehicles and anything else he had to pass on.

"I've just accepted a call to 27 Bloomfield Road, see a Mrs Woodhams re property found," he said.

"Yes thanks, we'll deal with that. Cheerio," I said as I slipped into the operator's seat.

"I be ready to whip old Blossom into action, young Dick, but where do I point 'er towards?"

I repeated the location and the reason for the call and we set off. Now it's funny to hear Ernie every now and then, but after a while his talking to the car as if it were an old cart-horse wears a bit thin. "Here we are then. Steady now, old gel. That's it, whoa there. OK, Dick, you go and see what she's found."

I walked up the path and knocked on the front door. Almost at once the door was thrown open and a woman aged about sixty rushed out of the door to greet me. It was quite obvious she was very upset. "Steady there my luv. What seems to be the matter, eh?" I asked. Blossom's way of speaking was affecting me already!

"It's my grandson and his mate. They found something in one of the old sheds on what used to be the allotments. It's revolting, that's what it is, revolting."

The word "revolting" conjured up all manner of ideas as to what it might be, ranging from obscene photographs to the carcass of a dead animal. None of my ideas came anywhere near what I found on the kitchen table when I was virtually pushed through the kitchen door.

In the kitchen stood two young boys aged about ten or eleven. "We ain't done nothink wrong, mister, 'onest we ain't, 'ave we 'Arry?" said the tallest of the two.

"No, we ain't. The shed was fallin' down any rate, warn't it?" came the reply from 'Arry.

"OK," I said. "We'll sort all that out in a minute. What did you find?"

"Nothink, just these," replied 'Arry, pulling away an old sack covering the objects on the kitchen table.

There, laying in the centre of the table were two adult human skulls and the right-hand half of a child's skull. "Where did you find these then?" I asked incredulously.

"You know where the allotments are be'ind Badgers wood? Well, we were up there playin' and we found an 'ut which was almost 'idden amongst all the blackberries and stinging nettles. We climbed in and found these and a lot of other bones," 'Arry told me, indicating the skulls on the table.

"D'yer think someone's been murdered?" enquired the other boy.

I went to the front door and called out to Blossom, "Bloss, get onto Information Room and ask them to get a Detective-Inspector down here as soon as possible. If he's not immediately available, get the Duty Officer."

"All right, Dick, I'll be in as soon as I've got through. You'll be OK then?"

"Yes, it's not going to run away." I then went back into the house and took particulars off the two boys and the informant.

About five minutes later, Blossom came to the door and said, "The DI says he's busy and can't come unless he's told what it's all about. The Duty Officer is taking a charge at St John's. What do you want me to do?"

"There's no way we can put this information over the radio. We'll have every reporter for miles around here within the hour if we do. Hold on a minute, Bloss." I went and found Mrs Woodhams and told her I was going to make a telephone call from the telephone box about a mile away and that I would be returning immediately afterwards.

"Don't you leave them revolting things on my kitchen table. Take them with you or something," she exclaimed.

"All right, I'll put them in the shed in the garden whilst I'm gone," I said. Then, turning to the two boys, I told them I wanted them to stand guard over the skulls until I came back. Neither of them must leave the garden.

I telephoned the Detective-Inspector from the telephone box and explained about the skulls and that according to the boys there were several more and other bones as well, but that we had not actually been to the locality before informing him. From his reactions you would have thought that there was a constant stream of victims being conveyed to the shed two or three times every day. He obviously had dreams of arresting a mass-murderer. I tried to explain to him that according to the boys there was no way into the shed other than through a small window which they could only just squeeze through. If I wanted to get in we would have to cut our way through the brambles and stinging nettles. Apparently, according to him, I did not know what I was talking about. He reminded me about what the Instruction Book told us to do as the first steps at the scene of the crime, one of which was that we should inform the CID as soon as possible. He then ordered that under no circumstances must we go anywhere near the shed and slammed down the 'phone. I went back to the car and told Blossom what had happened. He listened intently and said, "Orders be orders, Dick my lad. We'll go back and wait for him. Come on, Blossom, old gel. Walk on," and we returned to 27 Bloomfield Road.

Fifteen minutes later, over the brow of the hill came three cars in close formation. The first contained the Detective-Inspector, the Detective- Superintendent and a Detective-Sergeant who was their driver. The second car contained a Detective-Sergeant and two Detective-Constables. The third car, driven by a Detective-Constable, was full of shovels, spades, pick-axes, bagging-hooks, rope and heaven knows what else. They all screamed to a halt outside the front of the house, not because they were going all that fast but because the driver of the first car misread 23 for 27 and braked hard not to overshoot the address. The drivers of the two following cars almost had to make an emergency stop to avoid running into the back of one another. This all served to confirm what the neighbours in the street had already made up their minds about: old Mrs Woodhams had done away with her grandson and his friend and buried them in the back garden.

The Detective-Inspector came bustling along the pavement towards me, full of self-importance. I saluted him and told him that I had done nothing more but returned here. "Good, very good! It's a pity you can't work without supervision. Have to be told exactly what to do every step of the way, don't you? We'll deal with it from now on. We're the experts. Get back to looking for stray dogs."

I was furious but before I could say anything, Blossom grabbed me by the arm, spun me round and almost threw me into the car. He ran round to the driver's side, jumped in and set the car off at a gallop. As we drove along, he tried to calm me down. "Don't you go on so. That there silly idiot will get his come-uppance very soon. He's an incompetent fool, he makes them up as he goes along. You mark my words, he's going to look a bloody fool before this day's over."

By what we could gather from the Detective-Constables later, this is what happened. The whole of the detective squad had examined the skulls in the garden shed. They had taken the two boys to the location of their find. Here they had spent an hour searching for clues before cutting their way through to the shed. The door was so rotten that it collapsed as they touched it. Inside they found two more skulls, several other bones which were so badly chewed by dogs, rats, mice and foxes that it was impossible to tell if they were human or not, plus a very large pile of books on the subject of phrenology, the branch of science concerned with the localisation of function in the human brain. There were also several letters dated 1921 and addressed to Professor John Millard, care of Guy's Hospital, London.

Further research revealed that the ground had once been part of a large house which had been destroyed by bombing during the war and that it had never been used since. It became more and more obvious that no immediate crime had taken place and that the officers first on the scene should have investigated the whole thing, having first informed the Detective-Inspector as to the results of their findings; he should then have decided if it was necessary to waste the Detective-Superintendent's time or not.

The following week the Detective-Inspector was posted to Criminal Records Office in a supervisory capacity.

CHAPTER 7

In the modern day (some say enlightened) police force there is virtually no restriction on re-entering the station for any reason during a tour of duty. However, in my early police career it was a disciplinary offence to return to the station without a justifiable reason other than for the official refreshment period. A visiting officer must, on entering the station, report immediately to the Station Officer and sign the official book, stating time and reason. On leaving he had to enter the time and tell the Station Officer that he was going.

This created all manner of devious reasons being invented so that an officer could get back into the station around about the same time as the tea was being made. Some of the old-time coppers like "Dusty" Miller were masters at the art: bunches of keys found lying in the street; old broken watches; a single earring; an old purse (empty of course). All of these would have been collected from every known source within the family over the previous three months and held in reserve for use on a very cold or very wet night. On day duty these clever ploys were not nearly so necessary, as all the old-timers had their watering-holes. For a few it was the rear of one of the pubs, but mostly it was the friendly shop owner or assistant who brewed up regularly. These tricks and locations were jealously guarded and it was up to the new lad to find his own salvation.

Thank God! I thought. Only four more nights to go before the end of this tour of night duty. Two weeks, three days (or nights) and rain every night! No dry wireless car to sit in with the heater going this posting, just a foot beat which started about two miles from the station. Five shops, one small factory which made packing cases, a recreation ground and working-class terraced houses – hardly the beat where I was going to make any arrests for major crime offences. The best I could hope for was a drunk or a common assault. Although I had not done much service as yet, I had long since realised that the old saying "the best copper is heavy rain" was very true. This was the beat for the Walter Mitty approach to policing – the old tom-cat stalking an early- rising pigeon was really an armed robber creeping up on his victim, or the flickering light in the back of a shop was the owner, bound and gagged, operating the light-switch with his foot to send a morse-code SOS.

As I slowly plodded my way around the corner into Hartley Road I saw PC Tony Yorke coming towards me on the opposite side of the road. Tony was posted to number six beat which had Hartley Road as the mutual boundary with my beat.

"Hi, Tony. What a night! I swear it's colder than it's been all week."

"Sure is," replied Tony. "I wish I could find an excuse for a visit to the station. It's only twenty minutes to the time they make tea."

"Fat chance. Unless..." I said in a very slow and thoughtful voice. "Do you see what I see?" I pointed across the road. There, leaning against the short partition fence between the terraced houses were a lady's and a child's cycle. The front gate had long since disappeared and there was our passport to tea.

"We can't," said Tony in an incredulous voice, knowing full well we could, and would.

"We found them lying in the gutter just up the street, didn't we?" Tea! A warm nick! And a ride in as well! No sooner had I said it than I was striding across the road, followed reluctantly by Tony. "Here, you're smaller than I am, so you have the kid's bike," I said, pushing the smaller one in his general direction.

Tony took the bike; wheeled it into the roadway; held it away from him at arm's length and said, "Do you know, Dick, I used to have a bike exactly the same as this. Boy, did I use to do some tricks on it!" With that he sat on the seat backwards, took hold of the handlebars behind him, pushed off with his feet and travelled about ten yards before ending up in a heap in the middle of the road.

"That's nothing!" I said in a contemptuous voice. "How about this then?" So saying, I jumped astride my machine, pedalled a short distance, then climbed up so one foot was on the seat, the other up in

the air behind me whilst I held on to the handlebars with one hand. Slowly the cycle turned a full circle in the road before I made a rather ungainly dismounting. After all, a helmet, police raincoat and size ten boots were not exactly the attire for stunt riding.

"Not bad!" muttered Tony. "Can you do this?"

What "this" was, I never found out. Tony was just pushing his bike into the centre of the road when the quiet of the night was shattered by an upstairs bedroom window being flung open and a man's voice shouting, "When you two daft bloody clowns have finished, you can put my sodding bikes back."

The two cycles were thrown into the front garden and Tony and I took off in opposite directions as fast as we could run. When we booked off duty at six o'clock, we collected our own cycles from the cycle-rack in the station yard.

"Cheerio, Dick," called Tony. "This is what I was going to show you," he laughed, and with that he ran down the station yard and jumped astride his cycle. As he did so the flap of his raincoat caught in the front wheel, he pitched up into the air over the top of the handlebars and ended up in a big heap amongst the stray dogs tied to the kennel in the corner of the yard. The last sight of Tony, as I cycled out of the yard, was of him lying on the ground with a Labrador bitch sitting on his chest and licking his face. Sleep came very slowly that morning for me – it's difficult to go to sleep when you're still chuckling.

Night duty was often boring and there were fewer people around to observe, so it wasn't surprising that young probationers found ways of passing the time. Usually we made sure that these didn't come to the notice of Authority, so Tony Yorke and I felt hard done by when we got into hot water for another episode which looked like a prank, but wasn't.

For very nearly one hundred years, Ryford Market Square had smelled – not a nasty smell but one which depended very much on the direction of the wind as to which smell or combination of smells reached your nostrils as you walked along the pavement. There was the smell of beer coming from the cellars and doorways of the two pubs, the usual smells associated with greengrocery, the shoe shop, fish and chips, newly baked bread, roasting coffee and the smell of smouldering oak chippings from the curing sheds of the fishmonger's. High on the wall of the last establishment was a small plaque which declared that this was the site where one of Britain's most famous writers had been born. One sunny afternoon I was amazed to see two workmen equipped with a ladder remove the sign, cross the square and mount it on the wall of another shop.

This small incident was the start of changes which were to affect every High Street and shopping area in Britain. It was the prelude to the demolition of the building and the erection of one of the first-ever supermarkets in our country. Why Ryford had been chosen for such a revolutionary venture I do not know but its success, in spite of people's loathing of change, was startling. It was not long before and then other companies began to jump in to capture some of this rapidly expanding market. The so-called High Street Revolution had arrived and Ryford was to blame.

Most people are basically lazy, so it was not long after the supermarket opened that we police officers were confronted with two distinct problems. One which had always been around but which escalated with the opening of this revolutionary type of shopping was shoplifting. The second was far less important but nevertheless required police action: the leaving of trolleys in the streets where the customers' cars had been parked. The problem increased so much that within a year of opening, the store employed a youth to tour the vicinity, recovering the trolleys and returning them to the store. One of the most popular parking areas was Church Road, which led off the Market Square at one end and had a steep hill at the other. This hill was a one-in-five with two bends at the top, followed by over four hundred yards of straight road before it levelled out, crossing a small bridge over a stream at the bottom. Unlike the trolleys of today, the first trolleys had baskets at a much lower level and the two handles came up to normal height, rather similar to a sack- trolley with a basket in the front and four small wheels. These wheels were the same as today's, however, as they never went in the same direction at the same time and were built so that at least one did not rotate at all.

Hunching my shoulders, I retreated deeper into a shop doorway in an attempt to get out of the biting wind. It was the type of wind that my grandmother used to describe as a lazy wind. If asked why, she replied, "It's lazy because it won't go round you, only right through you." I could think of better places to be right now than Ryford

High Street patrol at 1 am on a February night. For example, there was the bedroom of the black-haired beauty who was the manageress of this shop; on the other hand, if I was there I could be in trouble but out here I was just cold. On reflection I knew where I would rather have been.

The sound of footsteps slowly making their way towards me up the High Street came to my ears. I altered my position so that I could see through the window display who the person was as they rounded the corner into Market Square. Within a minute Tony Yorke, who was posted number three patrol, came into view. Stepping out of the doorway, I greeted him with "Hi, there, Tony. Come on in and spend ten minutes having a natter and a fag."

"OK, Dick. I'm a bit early for grub," he replied. We entered the doorway and both squeezed into the deepest recess out of the wind, the proximity of our bodies making it a lot warmer. "Do you know, Dick, I would sooner be with the black-haired manageress of this shop, in here with no clothes on, than with you dressed in your best Sunday suit," laughed Tony.

I agreed, and for a moment we were both quiet whilst we had our own private thoughts. "It's a good job it's not an arrestable offence to think. Have you seen next month's postings yet?" I asked.

"Quiet!" hissed Tony. "Put your fag out. Someone's coming."

Obeying his orders, I strained my ears for any sound, then I heard the faint squelching sound of one-inch-thick crêpe-soled shoes. Slowly a youth, aged about eighteen and dressed in a light blue, double-breasted suit, yellow shirt and socks with blue creepers, came round the corner into the Market Square on the opposite side of the road to us. As we watched, he stopped at the cigarette machine in the doorway of the newsagent's directly opposite us. He turned, looked up and down the road and then reached inside his jacket and drew out a short jemmy. He again looked in both directions and then turned and started working on the machine with the jemmy. As quietly as possible, Tony and I eased our way to the opening of our doorway and stepped out onto the pavement. The youth stopped work for a moment and glanced up and down the road but not behind him, so he did not notice us. As we reached the centre of the road, Tony and I parted, he going to the left and I to the right. It was then the youth spotted me. "Stand still, you're under arrest!" I shouted, knowing full well that he wouldn't.

The youth turned away from me, only to find Tony coming from the other direction. He turned again and threw the jemmy at me. At

CIGARETTES
VICTORIA

the same time he started to run. With amazing speed, he turned the corner into Church Road with Tony and me in full pursuit in spite of our uniform. His flight was aided by the fear of capture and by the lightness of his clothing. How I wished I had achieve my ambition and had a police dog to release after him. By the time we reached the top of the hill, he was a good twenty yards up on us and drawing away. As he rounded the corner, he collided with one of the abandoned supermarket trolleys. He pitched head-first over the handles amd ended up half in, half out of the basket, feet in the air. The trolley bounced across the pavement, down the kerb and into the road, and started to gather speed as gravity took control. "We'll never get him now," I gasped.

"We'll get him. Jump on and hold tight." So saying, Tony grabbed the handles of another trolley and pushed it in my direction. He then grabbed yet another, scooted it into the roadway and jumped on as it gathered speed. Throwing caution to the wind, I did the same.

We were about half-way down the hill when I saw the headlights of a car coming towards us along the flat at the bottom of the hill. There was nothing any of us could do about it. The wheels of the trolleys were in control. Surprisingly, all three of us were keeping remarkably straight courses, with the youth easily some sixty yards in front of us. It was then that I suddenly realised that the car was being driven on dipped headlights. This, of course, meant the driver would not see leading trolley until the very last moment because of the steepness of the hill. I was right: just as the car was about to cross the bridge, the driver was confronted with a chromium-plated trolley, being driven by a maniac dressed in a blue suit, hurtling straight at him. The driver braked hard and swung to his nearside. He missed the parapet wall of the bridge, mounted the pavement, crashed through the iron railings and ended up nose first in the stream. The trolley hit the hump of the bridge, left the ground momentarily and overturned as it hit the roadway again, sending the youth sailing through the air to land about five yards further on.

What actually happened to Tony I don't know. I was much too busy with my own problems. I had no control at all over my trolley as it bounced and jumped all over the road. As I neared the bridge, I closed my eyes and prayed, bracing myself for the impact, but nothing happened. I felt the jolt as I crossed the hump of the bridge and very quickly became aware that I was slowing to a halt. I opened my eyes and tried to regain my feet which, for some inexplicable

reason, did not go where I wanted them to. Staggering across the road, I managed to catch hold of the youth just before he got up. At this, all thoughts of running left him and he sat in the roadway examining his torn suit and grazed knees. As I looked around me, I saw Tony emerging from the stream, his helmet held on the back of his neck by the chin-strap tight round his throat, his arms hanging by his sides, one of them at a very strange angle. He looked like the monster from the deep.

On the other side of the bridge, the rear of the car looked vaguely familiar. It was then that I saw Inspector Frank "General Custer" Hillier carefully climbing out of the offside door of the Duty Officer's car and up the bank of the stream. "All correct, sir," I reported as he crawled onto the roadway. "One arrest for attempted break-in of a cigarette machine, sir."

"You **** ****!"

"Sorry, sir, I didn't quite catch your reply. Would you repeat it, sir?"

"You **** **** ****!"

Parade book entry for Wednesday, 21st April: "It has come to my notice that Officers posted night duty are participating in a so-called "supermarket grand prix". Any Officer found participating in this dangerous activity will immediately be placed on a disciplinary charge and dealt with severely. Signed: Superintendent Banford."

It always seemed to be Tony Yorke who was my partner in these night duty escapades. Perhaps this was because I had led him astray on his very first night duty. For that particular occasion, though, we had needed a little help from our friends.

Tony had received all the necessary instruction from the Section Sergeant, who had walked out with him. Now he was on his own for the first time. To him I was an experienced police officer. Me, with the grand total of seven months and two days on the streets to my credit, an experienced officer? Still, in the land of the blind, the one-eyed man is king.

One thing I did know was that the back of any shop is always the most vulnerable, so not only must the fronts be checked to ensure that they were correctly secured but also the backs. On cold, wet, windy, pitch-black nights, the rear of the shops of Ryford High Street were no place for those with faint heart. It was claimed, justifiably, that some officers were too nervous to venture behind them, especially when one considers that to stand any chance of catching a wrong-doer, stealth and quiet were the order of the night.

The flashing of a torch could be seen hundreds of yards away. Probationer constables posted to the High Street patrol were therefore fair game for all manner of pranks. The most popular of these was for the beatman whose beat was superimposed over the High Street to provide the extra cover that such a high-risk area needed to get behind the shops by approaching over the rear fence from the park. Having hidden in a particularly dark area, he would then jump out in front of the probationer or say a loud "BOO!" just as he had crept by. Occasionally these shock tactics went very wrong. More than one beatman had suffered the pain of torn ears when the probationer, truncheon in hand, responded with the instinct of self-preservation on the helmet of his attacker.

So that night I was safely hidden in the outside toilet behind the shoe shop, waiting to do unto another that which had been done unto me. I strained my ears for the sounds of Tony's approach. Suddenly I held my breath. There was a noise, but it was the faint sound of a piano being played very quietly. That should never be! All the shops were lock-ups and the nearest house was at least four hundred yards away across the park. Easing myself from my hiding place, I crept slowly towards the sound.

The playing got more distinct, but not louder, as I neared its source. Then suddenly I could see the street lights shining through the shop and out of the open rear door of Davis's music shop. On reaching the open doorway I was able to see Tony Yorke seated in full uniform at a grand piano, playing exceptionally fine boogie. Giving a quiet cough, I entered the shop and was told by Tony that he had tested the rear door and it had opened. He had entered, carried out a quick search but found no one. Having discovered many years ago that he could play nearly any musical instrument by ear, he just could not resist playing the grand piano; after all, it was a Steinway.

I had a bit of music in my background, too, because for almost as long as I could remember, I had been interested in dancing, tap and modern ballroom being my forte. I had managed to pass my examinations and was of gold medal standard long before I had joined the police force. In addition I had discovered during my two years' National Service in the Royal Air Force that I had quite a respectable singing voice. In other words, a song and dance man. Mind you, it was always said that there was no such thing as a flop in a camp concert, service personnel being the easiest of all audiences to please. With this knowledge neatly filed away in my mind, my stage career

came to an abrupt end on that wonderful day when I was demobbed.

I located the telephone and rang into Ryford station, asking for the keyholder to be informed. I explained to Tony that it was the practice to stay at the premises until the keyholder arrived, providing that was not too long.

About ten minutes and five different tunes later, the wireless car pulled into the small lay-by about twenty yards past the shop. The crew of the car walked back and tapped on the front door of the shop. I unlatched the door, opened up and let them in.

"The keyholder says that as it's now 5.30 am he'll come in early, about 7.30, then he can stay on and open up at the usual time" instructed the car's wireless operator, PC Ted Brewer. "The Duty Officer says to close the door and keep casual observation on the shop until you go off duty. Hello! What's this then? I used to be quite a dab hand at the drums once upon a time." He slipped in behind the drum kit, picked up the brushes and quietly started beating out time on the kettle drum. Tony started to play the piano and I started a soft-shoe shuffle across the parquet floor. This was too much for the wireless car driver, "Blossom" Trevellyn. He lifted down a banjo and joined in. It was not very long before I was singing and dancing and saying "Do you know ...?"

After about fifteen minutes we realised that it was getting close to booking-off time. I bolted the back door and we all stepped out of the front door – to the sound of hand-clapping and the chinking of coins landing on the pavement. Directly across the road from the shop was the stop for the all- night bus, with the usual number of early-morning town workers waiting for the 5.58 am bus. It is quite amazing just how loud clapping sounds in an empty High Street at that time of the morning.

"Right, lads," whispered Ted Brewer. "Off helmets. Bow. Now, run like hell to the car and drive off quick!"

CHAPTER 8

Some police officers become a legend in their own service. This can be because of several acts of courage that they have performed, the jokes that they played on people, or their habit of being in the wrong place at the right time or vice versa. One such legend was Angus (not "Jock", unless you wanted to take the chance of having your ears pinned together) Macleod. Angus stood six feet two and a half inches in his stockinged feet and gave the appearance of being the same size in every other direction. Basically a quiet man, Angus was a master of driving and riding. It did not matter to Angus if it had two or four wheels as long as it had an engine. A mechanical conveyance to you or me, it was a living thing to him. He was reputed to have won his class in an Isle of Man TT race held after the war. Another story went that when he was on his test drive at the end of his course for a Class I police driver, he was asked to take the next roundabout a little faster. Angus is reputed to have approached the next roundabout at 70 miles per hour, gone into it at 60 and come out the other side at 55, much to the amazement of the examiner and the consternation of the back-seat passenger. And this was not one of the big open roundabouts built today but a little tight one on the Great West Road. For relaxation Angus bred geese.

"First time you and I have been posted together, isn't it?" asked Angus.

"Yes, J... er ... Angus," I replied.

"Right then, laddie, you had better know what I like and dislike. One, my name is Angus, not Jock. Two, I do not waste petrol driving around for nothing. If there is a call or something worthwhile, we will go, and go bloody fast, and I expect you to keep your finger on the bell the whole way. Three, I will have one or two small jobs to do during the next three weeks and you, laddie, will remember nothing about them, understand?"

"Yes, J... Angus," I murmured.

"It's nothing illegal, so don't worry that you're covering a crime. It's just using the transport available. Tomorrow, I want you to bring a civvy jacket with you. Don't ask why, you'll find out."

"OK, Angus."

Ryford was a sub-divisional station. This meant that it had three other stations in its area, all administered from Ryford. There were only two wireless or area cars, and they covered the whole sub-division between them. Situated on the edge of the Metropolitan Police District, Ryford sub-division bordered on two County Constabularies. The three sub-stations were named Axehurst, St John's and Hardborough.

5.45 was never a good time of the day for me. I stood bleary-eyed along with the rest of the relief, on parade for early turn. Briefings etc. over, Angus and I made our way to the brand-new (757 miles only on the clock) Wolseley 6/80.

"Got your civvy coat, laddie?" enquired Angus.

"Aye," I replied. Only one tour of duty so far and I was becoming affected. What will I speak like at the end of the three weeks? I wondered.

"Right then, we're awa' the noo."

Quietly the car purred along the road with Angus humming to himself whilst I wrote out the headings in the wireless log and car diary. I had just completed this task when the car came to a halt outside a smart semi-detached house. "OK, Dick, I'm just slipping indoors to fetch something, won't be a minute," smiled Angus.

When Angus returned I was busy logging a routine message about a lost or stolen car. I heard the boot-lid shut, then Angus opened the driver's door and slid into the seat, started the car and drove off. After we had travelled about two miles we had to stop at the traffic signals. That was when I became aware of a strange noise coming from the boot. "What's that noise?"

"Och! It's only a few wee goslings we're delivering," came the reply.

"Delivering where?"

"You'll find out. Come on, slip your tunic off and put on your civvy jacket," said Angus. Full of wonderment, I complied.

"All cars, all cars, lost or stolen since..." the message came over the radio. I entered it in the log and listed the details on the clip-board. When I had finished I looked up and, to my amazement, found that the car was easily five miles over the border into the County Constabulary area. The car flashed by a signboard and I just had time to read "Halchester 22½ miles." "Where the hell are we going? We're miles off our ground. If we get caught it's a discipline hearing without doubt," I shouted.

"Dinna worry, laddie. I've done this countless times over the years. Halchester is the market town and today is market day. My goslings are to be auctioned there. We'll just deliver them to the auctioneer and come straight back," said Angus. I was lost for words. It was all right for Angus: his family had grown up, his house was paid for and if he was required to resign he would still get his pension. Me, I had a wife, two kids, a police flat and nowhere to go when I sacked. The rotten b–.

The car sped on along the main road towards Halchester. "Always remember, laddie, if you behave in a way which looks as if you have a right to do what you are doing, ninety-nine per cent of the time you'll get away with it unchallenged," said Angus reassuringly.

If he had intended to quieten my fears, it did not work. I murmured, "What about the other one per cent?" but my question went unanswered.

On the outskirts of Halchester we began the two-mile downhill descent into the centre of the town. Halfway down the hill was a sharp right-hand bend. As it was market day there was quite a lot of traffic about, but it was moving OK. Just as we reached the bend a huge ginger tomcat shot out into the traffic, closely followed by a small mongrel dog which was not much larger than the cat. Angus swore as the driver of the car immediately in front of us stood on his brakes to avoid the animals. True to his reputation, Angus reacted instantly, braking and swerving towards the nearside kerb. He avoided the rear of the car in front and the Wolseley came to a stop. As it did so there was the most terrible crunching sound and jolting from the rear as a white Mark VII Jaguar smashed into the back of the wireless car.

My God! I thought. We've had it now for certain, there's no way we can talk our way out of this. "What the hell do we do now?" I shouted.

"Dinna worry, laddie, follow me," came Angus's calm reply. He

got out of the car, ran back and wrenched open the driver's door of the Jaguar. "Grab the passenger, Dick, don't let him get away," he shouted, as he reached into the car and dragged out the driver, a youth of about eighteen. I obeyed automatically and just managed to grab hold of the passenger as he attempted to pull himself up an eight-foot-high garden wall. Angus shouted at the driver, "Which car park did you take the car from, eh?"

"Hardborough railway station," came the reply. "How the hell did you know we'd nicked it?"

I dragged my prisoner back to the cars, but as I did so I was aware of strange noises all around me. Cackle, cackle, hiss, hiss. There were geese everywhere; in the road running amongst the traffic, on top of the cars, in fact all over the place. Feathers flying and wings flapping, they were most indignant about the way in which they had been released. The crash had sprung the boot-lid open and also burst two crates. Chaos reigned.

"Hey! You over there, telephone for the police," yelled Angus to a spectator. "Right, you two, into the back of our car and no trouble or else," he said threateningly. "As you get in, hand to us those two tunics." Nodding at me, Angus slipped into his tunic, just as the local constabulary wireless car came over the brow of the hill. "Quick! Get those two crates out of the boot, slide one just under our car and one under the front of the Jaguar," he told me quietly. "Hurry, Dick, they're almost here."

As the constabulary car screamed to a halt beside them, the geese, which had gathered themselves into a flock, were scattered in every direction once again. This gave Angus time to push the boot-lid down before the constabulary Sergeant got out of his car. "Where the hell did those geese come from?" he shouted.

"How do I know? We've got two arrests for taking and driving away this Jag. from our ground," replied Angus. "It would appear that there were a couple of crates of geese on the pavement right where we ended up. Who they belong to we don't know."

"Well, we'll have to round them up and get the traffic moving again," said the Sergeant. "Right lads, out of the car and help round up those geese," he said to his two officers.

"You help them, Angus, and I'll watch the prisoners," I said in a knowing voice. After about five minutes I was having to hold on to the side of the car because I was laughing so much at the great goose chase.

Six weeks later Angus and I stood together outside the Superintendent's office door, waiting to be called in. This was it, I thought. We're about to be told we are both placed on a discipline report. "Macleod, Kenyon, come in," came the voice from the Superintendent's office.

In we marched and stood to attention in front of the desk. "Ah, yes. Let me see now. Two arrests for taking and driving away a motor vehicle after a long chase," said the Superintendent. I was shaking. Here it comes, I thought. "Oh; stand easy. I'm pleased to be able to inform you that the District Commander has granted you both a commendation for determination and skill. Your records have been noted. Well done. That's all, dismissed."

Never has a cigarette tasted sweeter than the one I lit in the corridor outside the Superintendent's office. "Would you like to order a goose for Christmas, Dick?" said Angus, very assuredly, as he strolled off up the passageway.

Being a dour Scot, Angus hardly ever laughed. He was known to offer the occasional smirk at some of the better jokes, in various shades of blue, that went round the nick, but he had a real laugh only once or twice a year. Then it had to be something exceptional to set him off. If you heard his laugh, you knew why! No ordinary laugh for Angus: his laughs started somewhere down in the region of his feet, worked their way slowly up his body in a series of jerks, to arrive into the world eventually in the initial form of a strangulated, high-pitched squeak. This was closely followed by raucous laughter, which turned into a strange cackling noise every time he drew a breath. Angus laughed with his whole body.

Angus, I and several other officers were sitting in the police room of Ryford Magistrates' Court, waiting for our respective cases to be heard. As usual it was not long before someone asked, "Did you hear the one about...?" So started the usual round of joke-telling. Eventually I told a joke about a man with a very severe stutter, and the various adventures that befell him on his wedding night. It was a good story and I must have told it well, because the other officers, except Angus, laughed long and loud. Suddenly we all became aware of a strange rumbling, gurgling sound coming from the direction of Angus. We waited and suddenly his laugh erupted, swamping the room and spilling out into the hallway of the court.

"The officers in the case of John Henry King, PCs Kenyon and Macleod, they're bringing him up into court now," the voice on the loudspeaker in the police room said.

Angus was by this time almost beside himself. I rushed over to the drinking fountain in the corner of the room, soaked my handkerchief and smacked it firmly in the face of Angus, hoping that the shock of the cold water would silence him. On the contrary, it only made him worse. "Had to throw a bucket of cold water over them," he gurgled.

"Shut up, you bloody fool. We're on now!" I shouted, "Pull yourself together, we must go into court."

Angus wiped his face and tried and tried to stop. By the time we reached the swing doors into number one court-room, his laughter was reduced to a series of strangulated squeaks and heaving shoulders.

"John Henry King," read out the clerk of the court, "you are charged that on Thursday the 15th day of February, at .... How do you plead, guilty or not guilty?"

"G...g...g...g...uilty, sir," came the reply.

Until that moment Angus had been slowly subsiding but now, he was like a slightly uncorked bottle of lemonade which had been violently shaken. Hissing, gasping and getting redder by the second, Angus looked as though he was having a seizure.

"Is the officer unwell?" asked the Chairman of the Magistrates. "I will adjourn this case for twenty minutes so that he can receive medical attention."

"Thank you, Your Worship," I muttered. Stepping from the witness-box, I grabbed Angus and forced him through the swing doors into the corridor. With the doors still swinging to and fro, Angus exploded into the strangest series of sounds ever heard in Ryford Court.

Ten minutes later, the court usher came into the police room. "PC Kenyon, you are wanted in the magistrates' chamber," he said.

I straightened my tie, flicked the cigarette-ash from my tunic, wiped the toes of my boots on my opposite trouser-leg and tapped on the door of the chambers.

"Come in. Ah, officer, I sincerely hope that the other officer has recovered now?"

"Yes, thank you very much, sir. I have arranged for him to stay outside the court-room until such time as, and if, he is required to give evidence," I replied.

"Well, it must have been a very good joke for him to have ended up like that. What was it?"

When the case resumed, the Chairman exchanged a knowing glance with me as the defendant rose to address the court. "S... s... s... s...ir, I am v... v... v... v...ery s...s...s...s...orry," said John Henry King.

CHAPTER 9

Running a Magistrates' Court is one of the least glamorous branches of the police. Basically it is staffed by longer-serving officers who are on light duties with a few younger, fitter, officers who do the more strenuous work and deal with the prisoners. There is a variety of jobs to be done, a few of which are gaoler, summons-server, court usher, fine-taker and hearing-setter. These jobs are not all exciting in the normal way but are, of course, important as well as quite interesting. It is in court that you can hear all the facts of a case, not just part of the story.

My attachment to Ryford Court as part of my probationer training was very much routine until the last day. From the hearing list I had, I could see that the prison van should be fetching a prisoner from Brixton Prison for a further remand hearing. The prisoner had been charged with attempted murder of a police officer. I still remember the incident, which had happened about four weeks earlier. I had been posted to the wireless car with "Blossom" Trevellyn. We had received a call to a large, detached house standing in its own grounds on the corner of two roads at the so-called top or posh end of Ryford. The call had been silent-alarm activated by suspects on premises. These alarms registered in the information room at New Scotland Yard without making a sound on the actual premises. We could not have been further away, right on the other side of our area. Whipping Blossom into a full charging gallop, we sped across the ground, bell sounding all the way: no sirens in those days, only a push-button on the dashboard to sound a large bell.

The "Q" car, a plain-clothed, nondescript, CID-manned car had been only a mile away when the call came out. They rushed to the scene, the crew splitting up in an effort to cover all sides of the house whilst waiting for assistance before searching. Suddenly a man burst out of a window on the ground floor at the rear of the house and ran across the garden and over the fence into a side road. One of the CID officers immediately gave chase. They climbed over a fence and the chase continued down the roadway. All at once the suspect stopped, turned and deliberately took aim with a revolver at the closing officer. At very close range he fired, and the bullet smashed its way through the officer's teeth and lower jaw before lodging itself deep in his throat, resting against his spine. In spite of his wound, the officer threw himself at the suspect, grabbing hold of his jacket. The struggle was very one-sided and the suspect slipped out of his jacket and made good his escape.

A few days later, officers of the Flying Squad raided a house in North London, bursting into the bedroom of the suspect and disarming him before arresting him. All officers received £15 from the Bow Street Award Fund and the injured officer eventually received the George Cross for bravery.

With the injured officer still on the critical list and fighting for his life, security surrounding the prisoner at Ryford Court was intense, though nothing at all in comparison with the standards we hear of nowadays. The prisoner arrived handcuffed to two officers and the walk from the prison van across the yard and into the court cells was kept to a minimum. Every policeman in the court that day could have willingly administered his own form of punishment, and all eyes were naturally focused on this prisoner.

Being on attachment meant that I had been given the job of warning the officers in the police room as to which case was to be heard next. This morning the police room was empty, with every officer squeezed into number one court to hear the remand proceedings. I made my way to number one court with the intention of warning two officers that their case was just coming on in number two court. As I walked down the corridor, the swing doors of number two court burst open, the nearer one hitting me in the face and chest. The force of the impact knocked me backwards to the floor, my nose streaming blood and tears filling my eyes. I vaguely remember being trod on by whoever came through the doors, and the sounds of shouting and running feet. As fast as I attempted to stand up, the swing doors were thrown open, knocking me to the ground again, and I was then trampled on once more. After three attempts to stand up, I decided to roll to the other side of the corridor, away from number two court. This I did and had just managed to regain my feet when the doors of number one court crashed open, knocking me to the floor again. This time there was a long stream of people rushing through the doors, half of whom succeeded in trampling on me.

Eventually I felt myself being lifted to my feet and being assisted to the court staff-room. From there I was taken to hospital to have my nose and chest X-rayed. Luckily no bones were broken, but I did have a pair of black eyes and bruising to my body. Apparently, with all the police officers present concentrating on the attempted murder prisoner, security of the other prisoners had been lax.

My initial knock-down had been caused by a prisoner who suddenly saw his chance to escape; he had run up the dock steps from the cell passage below, jumped the dock railing and burst out through the swing doors. All the subsequent batterings were caused by police officers joining in the chase. The escapee was recaptured about two hundred yards from the court when he ran into the courtyard of the Council offices, only to discover that all doors into the buildings were locked. I certainly left my mark in Ryford Magistrates' Court: a chip out of the woodwork on the swing doors into number two court.

Very occasionally, it was necessary for an officer to attend a Magistrates Court in order to give evidence, in another part of the Metropolitan Police District. The differences between them were, and still are, very striking.

If you went to any inner London court where the stipendiary magistrates sat, you would find all the previous night's drunks who were pleading guilty lined up in a cell passage under the court. As each defendant's name was called, he and the officer involved would mount the steps into the dock together. The officer left the dock and made his way round to the witness-box. During this short time the clerk of the court had read out the charge and the defendant had pleaded. The magistrate looked towards the witness-box and the officer would step up on one leg, half in and half out, and say, "No trouble, Your Worship", or "Urinating in a shop doorway, Your Worship", or "Unconscious on the footway, Your Worship", depending on the charge. Then, whilst the officer returned to the box, the Court Inspector read out the previous convictions and the Magistrate doled out the fine, finishing at just about the same time as the officer reached the defendant to take him downstairs again, squeezing past the next in line who were on their way up. Time for the whole episode? Two to three minutes at the outside, sometimes even quicker.

In the outer divisions, where the courts have a bench of magistrates, the whole thing took on a degree of farce by comparison. They always required the full details of the time and place, what the defendant was doing or not doing, whether his speech was slurred and whether he smelt of alcohol, etc. Time taken: five to fifteen minutes, depending how vocal the defendant was. In each case, justice was dispensed according to the requirements of the area. In most cases, the fines also reflected the affluence of the defendant and of the area: five shillings in the Inner London Courts as opposed to ten or even fifteen shillings which was normal in Ryford.

I well remember taking a prisoner by van to Vine Street late one night. As I was leaving, the door into the charge-room burst open and a police constable hurtled backwards on his heels across the room and hit the far wall, sliding gracefully to the floor. Uttering a few suitable oaths, which brought into doubt the perpetrator's parentage, he then jumped up and ran back out into the station yard. The next instant a rather large red-headed Scot, complete with kilt, followed exactly the same path as the officer had thirty seconds earlier. The only difference this time was that Jock did not jump up, he just sat there singing "Annie Laurie" at the top of his voice. The following morning at court I was amazed to hear, "No trouble. Your Worship" from the same officer, who was by this time sporting a lightly blueing right eye.

My most unconventional meeting with the Chairman of the Ryford Magistrates started with what I thought was going to be a simple booking for a parking offence. Contrary to popular belief, there is no way a constable is able to gain promotion based on the amount of work he has done. If it was true, I could think of a number of little Hitlers who would be vying for the rank of Commissioner of Police; it was, and still is, a sad fact that a few police officers consider themselves to be dictators of all they survey both on and off duty. I have even known some of them who were not averse to reporting people for parking offences, even though they were off-duty and in plain clothes. This type of policeman tends to give all of us a bad name. It is impossible to remember just how many motorists, when I reported them for motoring offences, replied with sneers to the effect, "One more towards your Sergeant's stripe, eh?",

"Wouldn't you be better employed catching criminals instead of harassing the poor motorists?", or "Persecuting the poor motorist yet again?" These remarks and others in similar vein tended to upset me until I overheard old "Dusty" Miller dealing with a lady motorist who had just used the "catching the criminal" retort to him. "Well, madam", he said, "if only you would park your car in the car park and not in a restricted street, then I would have more time to do just that." He said it in such a way she could not take offence. This response I used very often from then on. For me, reporting traffic offences was a part of the job which had to be done. I did not like it, just as I disliked dealing with accidents, deaths and many aspects of police work. However, there were some motoring offences over which I had no hesitation in taking as much action as possible. The main ones were no insurance and drunk in charge of a motor vehicle, closely followed by dangerous, reckless or careless driving.

Although unable to gain promotion by reporting motorists, I soon discovered that everyone from Sergeant upwards expected a probationary constable to turn in a certain amount of work each week. Arrests for various offences were great – when they could be found. Ryford was not like some of the inner divisions where a probationer had only to walk out of the station to get himself a drunk or a down-and-out or something which was rather minor but still proved that he was in fact working. But motoring offences were readily available in Ryford and in those days it was quite amazing just how quickly the word got round with the regular motorists in the area that a keen probationer was on duty that week. He only had to walk slowly in an area to be greeted by motorists running back to their parked cars calling "Just going, officer", or "Only been there a minute". This was a great way to keep traffic flowing but no good if the officer was short of work that week. If he was short he would adopt different methods, so that he suddenly appeared in the middle of a particular area without having walked through it. Usually, this was achieved by walking along the rear of shops or entering via a side street. Sometimes the effect of doing this was quite dramatic, especially if he managed to stand in a shop doorway where he could observe the street without being seen. I had adopted this ploy on several occasions, but there was an art to stepping out at just the right moment. Too early, and the motorist would veer away from the car and enter a shop where they would wait, hoping you would go away; too late, and they were in the car and driving away before you were in a position to speak to them. Many has been the time when the motorist and I have actually run towards the car in an attempt to beat the other. On one particular occasion I got far more than I had bargained for.

In 1956, there were still a large number of pre-war cars on the streets. Many were in superb condition, whilst others created the impression that if stopped once the owner had managed to get them running, they would suffer a horrible death right there in front of you in the middle of the road. In fact, it was always a very good practice to avoid stopping one of these types of car when you were on point duty. Far better to make the stationary traffic wait an extra thirty seconds so that a just mobile vehicle cleared a junction than to stop it and risk it stalling. Many is the time I have seen policemen pushing stalled cars clear of junctions.

On one particularly beautiful spring morning, I was waiting in a shop doorway for the return of a motorist who had parked a 1937 Wolseley saloon in a yellow banned area. It was parked with its driver's door closest to the kerb, facing away from me and about thirty yards distant. Things were getting desperate; here it was, Friday morning, and so far this week all I had to show for a week's work were two seventeen-year-olds, summonsed for riding pedal cycles at speed on the pavement through a crowd of shoppers. I had waited for about twenty-five minutes when, whilst giving directions to the nearest Ladies for a harassed mother with a three-year-old little girl who, from the way she was hopping up and down clutching herself, was never going to make it, I noticed a woman just climbing into the driver's seat of the Wolesley. Now, a pre-war Wolseley's doors are hinged on the centre post, so most details of the person getting into the car were hidden from me behind the open door, as, of course, I was to them. All I could see was that the driver was female.

I walked quickly along the pavement, reached the door of the car before it closed, and said, "Excuse me, madam, is this your car?"

"Oh! My God! You frightened me. Oh! No! Not now! Please not now!" Before I could say or do anything, she clutched her stomach and her face screwed up in pain. I then saw that she was heavily pregnant. I also noticed the wet stain slowly spreading over her skirt and over the seat of the car. "My baby, it's coming, officer. Please help me." So saying, she grabbed hold of my left hand, squeezed so hard that I swear the bones were misplaced, and held on.

I frantically tried to remember what I had done when my wife's waters had broken and what I had been taught in first aid classes.

That's right – call for an ambulance and make the patient as comfortable as possible. Call for an ambulance was great, but how? There was no way the woman was going to let go of my hand and, by the way she kept tightening her grip at such short intervals, there wasn't much time, either. "You ladies over there!" I shouted to a group of women at a bus stop on the opposite side of the road. "Can anyone help me? This lady is having her baby. Please phone for an ambulance as well."

" 'Old on, mate," came a cockney voice from the queue. "Ada, you get on the dog and bone in that there shop and call for the meat wagon. Come on the rest of yer, come and 'elp the poor cow." With that, one woman stepped off the kerb, turned and faced the queue. "Come on then, move yer bleedin' selves." I heard her call out. Within seconds, I was surrounded by women. "Gawd blimey, ain't yer got 'er drawers orf yet? Poor little bleeder'll never get 'ere tryin' to get through the gusset."

"I'm very sorry about this, my dear, but I will have to take your knickers off." I said apologetically.

"I don't care what you do," came the reply.

As I struggled to remove her knickers with one hand, I became aware that I could feel that there was a rounded form between her thighs. There was nothing I could do but support the child's head. "Will you hold her hand, luv, whilst I try to support the baby?" I said to that wonderful cockney lady.

"Course I will, luv. Do you know what to do?"

"I'm not certain but I'm sure nature will work things out," I said.

"Work things out? Work things out? Gawd, you're a caution. You're only a bleedin' kid yerself, but you've got a sense of 'umour. If you get into trouble down there, yell out. I've 'ad six of the little sods, so I know a bit about it. You married mate?"

"Yes, but what's that got to do with it?"

"Well, don't tell yer old girl that you've 'ad yer 'ands up another woman's clouts or you'll be divorced," she chortled. "It's all right, gal, you rest a mo'. That's it, steady now, right, grip 'old of me 'ands tight, go on, as tight as yer like, luv. How yer doin' down that end, mate?"

"OK, one more push and it should be here."

Suddenly, from out of the crowd, fluttered two brand-new bath towels and a voice said, "Wrap it in these."

"Thanks. Steady, steady, my dear, push, steady, you've almost done it."

"Yeah, don't rush it, gal, push when you need to," said the cockney lady. "That's it, luv, now push. Look out down there, cock, 'cause it'll be out like a bleedin' cork out of a bottle any second."

In actual fact, the baby just gently slipped free. I knew enough to wipe its nose and mouth clean; then I held it up by its heels and slapped its bottom twice. The second slap did it: with a big gulp of air, the child began to breathe and let out a scream. I gently wrapped it up and gave it to its mother. Then I looked around me. The car, the driver and I were surrounded by a circle of women, all with their top coats off, holding them out in front of them to form a screen. The cockney lady turned out to be a big brassy blonde, aged about fifty.

"Thank you very much," I said to her, "and also all you other ladies."

"Gawd luv us, that's all right, me old cock. Only too 'appy, ain't we, gals?"

"Let us through, please, make way there," came a voice from the back of the crowd. The screen parted and the ambulance crew pushed their way through. "There we are, my love, gently does it. We'll soon have you in the maternity hospital," said one of them to the mother.

"Thank you all so very much for all that you did, especially you, officer, and you, lady," she said. With that she was lifted onto the stretcher and taken to the ambulance.

"Well, what was it?" asked a voice from the crowd.

"It was a boy," I replied in a loud voice. At the news, a little cheer went up and the crowd began to drift away. "Just a minute, could I have your name and address for my report?" I said to the brassy blonde.

"Can't stop, luv, 'ere comes me bus. Come on, Ada, or we'll miss the bleeder. Cheerio, mate." So saying, the two of them ran across the road and boarded the bus. As it pulled away they gave me a wave, and that was the last I ever saw of them.

The details of getting the pavement washed down, the car removed and the report made out are all a matter of routine. However, the subject which was not routine and created threats of disciplinary action for losing police property was my missing helmet. Somehow, during the half-hour while I had been busy introducing a new being into our crazy world, my helmet disappeared. I vaguely remembered removing it at the start of my groping between the woman's thighs. I

remembered thinking to myself, get rid of your bloody helmet, you look bad enough without it on, heaven knows what she will think with that bobbing up and down there. That was the last I had seen of it. Enquiries made of the bystanders only revealed a wag at the back who commented that he had seen a dog running off with something and another who had definitely seen some kids playing football with it. At a time when it was the "in thing" to have displayed on your bedroom wall a trophy of some sort or the other, it was not very hard to realise what had happened to it. Street name-boards, no waiting, no entry, halt and slow signs and anything else which could be acquired were much prized and were supposed to prove just how "daring" the possessor had been in obtaining it. No matter how aggrieved I felt, it was decided by my senior officers that I should be assessed for the cost of replacement. Luckily it was decided that in the circumstances, I should not be placed on a discipline report.

Some weeks later, I stood in the back of St Peter's and St Paul's Church in full uniform. "In the name of the Son and the Holy Father, I name you Richard Kenyon David St John." Poor little sod, I thought.

"My husband and I would be very pleased if you could return home with us for a piece of christening cake and to wet Richard's head," said Mrs Monica St John, who was a good-looking, well-proportioned young woman in her late twenties.

"That's very kind of you. I'll be delighted to accept," I said, pleased.

The house was one of the upper-middle-class ones on the edge of town, and the christening tea reflected this with champagne, smoked salmon and the trimmings. As I walked into the room where it was being served, I was amazed to see the familiar face of the Chairman of the Magistrates. "I expect you've met my father, haven't you?" enquired Mrs St John.

When the christening cake was wheeled in on a trolley, it was in the shape of a police helmet, correct in every detail. After the inevitable photographs of myself with young Richard and, of course, the cake, I made my excuses and prepared to leave. I had just reached the hallway and was searching for my helmet amongst all the other hats and coats when the Chairman of the Magistrates approached me. "Ah, there you are, officer. Here is your helmet and also one we found jammed under the front seat of my daughter's Wolseley when we got it home. Sorry for not returning it before but we kept it so we could get the cake looking exactly right. Hope you don't mind."

I was very excited by the prospect of doing my attachment with a dog-handler. At last, this was going to be my chance to gain experience with a police dog. Among other things I would act as a criminal for the dog, something that all handlers had to do for one another's dogs. In this way not only would I be able to learn a lot of the things a dog could do, but also what to expect should I ever be lucky enough to be selected for dog-handling duties. Dog-handlers perform only a seven-hour tour of duty each day, the other hour being designated for grooming, feeding and exercising the dog at home. I was therefore very surprised when I was warned to work from 1 am to 11 pm every day for a week with Harry Sanderson, the handler from Axehurst who was on loan to Ryford due to our own handler

being in Cyprus. I met Harry on the Monday afternoon in Ryford front office when I booked on duty.

"Right, my name is Harry and my dog's name is Teddy. Sorry about the name but that's the one he had when we got him. Come on, let me introduce you to him. After all, if we're working together he'd better know you're on our side." With this, Harry led me downstairs to the basement where, lying in a corner with his lead looped over the top of a radiator, was the biggest dog I had ever seen. As we entered the room Teddy stood up and shook himself, wagging his tail at the same time. Teddy was three years old and fully grown. He must have stood 28 inches to the shoulder and weighed 125 pounds. He had a long, fluffy brindle coat and his head was smooth-coated except for his ears. His tail was nothing more than an apology for a tail. One would have expected it to be large and fluffy like his body, but because of recurring eczema, it could only be compared with that of a rat. In spite of his strange looks, Teddy had earned himself quite a reputation. No longer did the yobs on the High Street jeer at Teddy, and a large number of criminals had lost their liberty due to him.

Harry bent down and released Teddy and told him to come and make friends with me. This was an experience long to be remembered. Teddy ambled over to me and started by smelling my shoes and then slowly working his way up me. Finally he rose up on his hind legs and placed his huge paws, one on each shoulder, and licked my face. I staggered under his weight and was relieved when he reverted to his rightful place on the floor.

"That's OK, then. He'll know you now," assured Harry. "By the way, do you like going to the cinema?"

"Yes, the wife and I usually go once a week if we can," I replied.

"That's good because that's what we're going to be doing all week. We are doing ten-hour shifts to cover both afternoon and evening showing of a film. Come on, let's go."

When the producers of a film entitled *The Blackboard Jungle*

introduced a small scene of an American rock'n'roll band into the film, they had no idea what they had started. This short sequence was greeted with enthusiasm by the younger generation. So great was it, that the makers hurriedly shot another "B"-rated, film which had a very poor plot, if any at all, but did feature Bill Haley and the Comets. The film was entitled *Rock around the Clock*. Its effect on the youth of Britain was amazing. It was as if a cork had been removed from a bottle, releasing its previously shaken contents. Wherever the film was showing, teenagers jumped up and started dancing (if jiving can be classed as dancing – whatever it was, I enjoyed doing it). The trouble was that they caused quite a bit of damage to the cinema seats and upset other cinema-goers. Police were called to nearly every showing of the film. Now the film had been re-released to coincide with a personal tour of Britain by Bill Haley and the Comets. In an effort to forstall any trouble, wherever possible a dog-handler and another constable were posted inside the cinema while the film was showing. However, it was soon discovered that such was the build-up of excitement among the teenagers that they were jiving in the aisles before the actual film came on, so we had to spend the whole time there.

The whole basis of dog training is built around repetition; associating a command with a particular action. It therefore took only two days for Teddy to realise that whenever rock'n'roll music was played, he was ordered to show aggression towards the teenagers who were dancing. By the time of the last showing on Tuesday evening, Teddy was transformed into a snarling machine, even though he could not see anyone dancing from his position. By the end of the week Teddy only had to hear a few bars of rock'n'roll music and he would be transformed. The problem was, of course, that the rock'n'roll era had been born and the music was being played everywhere, not just on records and on the radio but also through the skiffle groups which appeared almost spontaneously overnight. It was very much a do-it-yourself, cheap and mainly working-class pastime. After all, a skiffle group could be created out of a wash-board, a cymbal, a double bass from a tea-chest, broom - stick and string and one or more guitars (the only really expensive item). Indeed, many police stations created quite successful skiffle groups who performed for charity.

On the Saturday night we were sent to aid Lewisham. It was here, at the Gaumont cinema, that Bill Haley made one of his personal appearances. Well over a thousand teenagers converged on Lewisham, whether they had tickets or not. Those who could not get in crowded around the outside of the cinema, blocking the road, all hoping to see their idols and to hear some of the music. Many had also brought their skiffle instruments with them and started playing. The crowd immediately around them started to jive. The net result was what has been dubbed the Rock'n'Roll Riots. In the light of what Britain has witnessed in the past few years, a better term to have used could have been a Rock'n'Roll Mêlée or Affray. There were a few fights and scuffles with the police as we tried to clear the road for traffic. Eventually, six or seven dog-handlers formed up across the road facing the crowd then advanced, together with their dogs on leather collars and short leads. Entering the crowd about three or four yards, they turned and drove the teenagers out in front of them. We stood in a line, waiting to swoop on any who did not take the hint and disperse peacefully or who were indulging in some other arrestable pastime. Within the hour, most of the crowd had been dispersed and the few that were left required little policing. I had witnessed a truly practical demonstration of the usefulness of police dogs deployed in the right way. Harry and I were presented with free passes which would admit two adults by the grateful management of the Gaumont cinema, Lewisham. A very nice gesture except that about ten months later they closed it down and sold the building.

One Saturday afternoon about a year later, Harry and Teddy were patrolling Ryford High Street. One of the shops was Stone's Radio Stores, which was part of a chain of shops throughout England. A feature of their sales technique was to play music in their doorways so that the public would be attracted by the sound. Just as Harry and his dog drew level with the doorway, the sound of "One o'clock, two o'clock, three o'clock, Rock" suddenly began to blare out. In an instant Harry had on the end of the lead a snarling ball of fur which was intent on biting every innocent pedestrian in sight. Jerking on the lead, Harry managed to get the dog under control, but not before there had been several near-misses – it is not only elephants that never forget.

The rock'n'roll age was also the heyday of the coffee bars. Where have they all gone? In the 'fifties and 'sixties they were the places where all teenagers congregated. No self-respecting town would have less than two or three spaced out along its main street. There were three major attractions to be found at any one of them: espresso coffee, the juke box, and teenage girls in the multi-petticoated flared

skirts and tight jumpers. What more could any self-respecting teenage youth want in life, after he had bedecked himself in the latest fashion of double-breasted, single-buttoned, brightly coloured suit with black collar, "slim jim" tie and brothel-creeper shoes, not forgetting the "DA" or "Boston" haircut. The nearest thing today that could be said to vaguely resemble those coffee bars would be a Wimpey or McDonalds, but these fast-food shops could never match the very special atmosphere of the coffee bars. Certainly Bic's Coffee Bar was a thriving feature of Ryford High Street.

"Right, lads. As you all know, in the last five weeks there have been seven safe-blowings down the High Street. Whoever this team is, they are getting too confident and sooner or later they are going to get nabbed. The CID boys aren't getting anywhere, so let's make it this relief who feel their collars. The governors believe that extra men on the High Street will deter them. So one, two, three, four and five beats will travel to their beats via the High Street on their way out. Six to ten beats will return to their beats via the High Street after grub." These were the instructions of the Section Sergeant as he paraded us for our first night duty of the three-week tour.

For the next five nights the orders were the same. Ryford High Street had more coppers travelling up and down it than patrolled the grounds of Buckingham Palace. The local teddy boys and hangers-on just didn't know where to go next to escape the attentions of us all. Normally they moved around in small groups of six to ten and basically gave little trouble. There was the occasional flare-up if some outsiders arrived to "sus out the local talent", but the continual presence of coppers who moved them on if they as much as stopped to light a cigarette was causing them all to seek refuge in Bic's Coffee Bar. This was great for trade but it brought more "Teds" into one place at the same time and for longer than normal. Sooner or later there was bound to be trouble, but at least there had been no break-ins so far.

Saturday night was usually the busiest night on the High Street. Ryford High Street had three cinemas, one theatre, seven pubs and the one late-night coffee bar, all turning out within roughly half an hour of one another. This created the minimum amount of trouble providing the normal patrolmen made sure that they were capable of being seen and that the small groups which stopped talking on the pavement did not stay too long or grow too large. The Duty Officer, Inspector Wilf Wilburn, was an old-timer who was in the last year of his service. He was wise to the ways of the yobs and could foresee trouble which was building up as a result of the extra attention we were giving to the High Street. It was obvious to us all that if trouble did come, it would be on either Saturday or Sunday night.

"All beat men will travel to and from their beats via the High Street tonight. Try to stagger your times there by spreading out and making your way via the side streets and alleyways. We think tonight will be the trouble night," ordered the Inspector as we paraded for duty on Saturday night.

I left the station and walked slowly down Lovers Lane, an alleyway which was well named as there were no street lamps in it at all. I have often wondered just how many of Ryford's residents were actually spawned in this alleyway. By the number of couples who scuttle away when you walk down it, quite a large number I should think. I made my way up Station Approach and into the railway station forecourt. From there I could see Bic's Coffee Bar, the Gaumont cinema, the Bricklayer's Arms and five bus stops. Initially all appeared normal. There were the couples who had spent a lecherous three hours in the back rows of the cinema, gazing into one another's eyes as they waited for the bus to take them to their respective homes; there were the married couples who stood and talked or said nothing to one another whilst they waited in the same queue. The various pub regulars ranged from retired couples who had been out for their regular pint and sing-song to the lonely middle-aged men and women who went to the pubs solely for companionship.

Suddenly I realised that there was something wrong. Bic's was empty except for two young girls who sat quietly, sipping espresso coffee. Normally one would expect to find maybe twenty or so of the local "Teds" and yobs in there, but because of the extra policing this week, I would have thought there should have been nearer fifty. Slowly I made my way across the road and to the back of the café. This was one of my regular tea or coffee stops and Marie, the manageress, was only too pleased to have the presence of a policeman as added protection for her in a potentially dangerous job. (Her pleasure at having policemen calling at the back door of the café extended well after closing time whenever one particular officer was on duty, but that is another story.) I opened the rear door, poked my head around it and said "Good evening Marie. Where is everybody?"

" 'Allo, Dick. What will it be, the usual? B–d if I know where they all are. All this week I've been packed out, but tonight, nobody!"

"Are these two regulars?" I asked, pointing at the two young girls.

"Yes, they're always in here. Sometimes I wonder if they've got homes to go to."

"Right, let's see if they know where everybody has got to." I made my way through the small kitchen and into the coffee bar. The two girls almost fell off their seats when I appeared from behind the counter. "Evening girls. Where is everyone tonight?" I enquired.

"Don't know, do we?" came the reply.

"Come on, you can do better than that. You know where they are, don't you?" This was met with a stony silence. I turned my back on the girls and said to Marie, "Marie, phone the nick for me, will you, and ask for the WPC to attend here to find out what these two thirteen-year-olds are doing out at this time of night."

Before Marie could answer, a voice from behind me protested. "We're both seventeen ain't we?"

Winking at Marie, I slowly turned to face the girls again. "Seventeen? Never! More like thirteen or fourteen," I said.

"All right, they've gorn up to New Cross to have a bundle with the local mob up there. We ain't got no money for the train fare so we 'ad to stay 'ere. C'mon Sandy, let's go before 'e calls that bleedin' cow of a woman copper down 'ere." Grabbing her make-up case from the table, the girl and her companion got up and left.

I telephoned the station so that they could pass the information to Deptford and warn them of possible trouble. It was too late: the rival mobs had met outside New Cross Gate railway station and had set to with a will. In all, thirty-seven were arrested for various offences including offensive weapons, various degrees of assault and insulting words and behaviour.

Having finished my coffee, I made my way slowly out to my beat. As I rounded the corner into Carterton road, I thought I glimpsed the flash of torch-light inside the Co-op stores. I immediately stopped and slowly eased my way into the deep shadows cast by the end wall of the cycle shop opposite. I waited nearly two minutes for another sign to confirm my suspicions and had just made up my mind that I must have been mistaken when it came again. As quietly as possible, I made my way back around the corner out of sight of the shop and stood trying to remember where the nearest telephone box was, other than the one outside the Co-op which I obviously couldn't use. The next one was over half a mile away. I had just made up my mind that I would have to go it alone as it was certain they would be gone by the time I got to the telephone, made a call and returned to the scene, when I saw the headlights of a car coming down the road towards me. I stepped into the road, flashed my torch two or three times in the direction of the car and held up my hand for it to stop. To my amazement, instead of slowing, the driver of the car changed down a gear and accelerated straight towards me. I flashed my torch again and moved it backwards and forwards across my body. Still the car came closer, gaining speed. I had almost decided to jump aside when the nos of the car suddenly tilted forward and the tyre squealed on the road as the driver braked hard. As the car slowed and came to a halt, I heard the familiar voice of "Blossom" Trevellyn saying, "Whoa there, Blossom, steady now," then laughing and saying, "Oi nearly 'ad you there, me old dear, B-d if I didn't. It's old Blossom 'ere, she don't like lights shone into 'er eyes. She always bolts when that there 'appens to 'er, she does. What's the matter then, Dick?"

"You bloody fool, you could have killed me," I said.

"No fear of that, my dear. Old Blossom 'ere would never step on a 'uman, but may be in your case."

"Shut up, you idiot, I've just spotted suspects on premises at the Co-op around the corner." Quickly I told Blossom and his operator, Bill Evans, what I had seen. Bill was chortling and I suspected that pretending to run me down was his idea of a joke.

"OK, my dear, I'll tie old Blossom up to that there lamp post, give 'er 'er nose bag and we goes and sees what you've found. Come on,

Blossom, steady now, me old darling." He moved the car into the side of the road, switched off the engine and lights, got out and quietly closed the door.

Carefully we edged our way around the corner and, using as much shadow as we could find, made our way towards the Co-op stores. Using hand signals we decided to split up: Bill Evans was to go to the front door whilst Blossom and I would take the rear. Just then there was a muffled but very large explosion inside the shop, accompanied by a bright orange flash. An instant later, the front windows of the shop burst outwards, showering glass all over the pavement. Luckily we had been pressed to the wall to avoid being seen, so escaped injury. Before we could say or do anything, a figure dressed in dark blue overalls staggered backwards out of the hole where the door of the shop had once been. It had both hands clutched to its face and blood was oozing through the fingers. From inside the shop came muffled screams.

Bill Evans dived across the pavement and grabbed the injured suspect, whilst Blossom and I entered the shop together. The sight that greeted us was reminiscent of the bombing during the war. One side of the shop was untouched, whilst the other was utter destruction. There was not a single item that was not smashed almost beyond recognition. Fluttering slowly to the floor amongst all the dust and rubbish were hundreds of one-pound and ten-shilling notes. They were just like flakes of confetti, only larger.

We followed the sounds of the screams and found that they were coming from what had been the manager's office, according to the sign which hung limply on a short piece of chain from a hook above what had once been the doorway. Exactly where the screams were coming from was difficult to establish in all the dust and smoke. As I stepped forward to enter the office, I trod on the steel door of a large safe. At once the screams became louder and I immediately stepped back, but the floor felt spongy. I shone my torch downwards and discovered I was standing on an arm which disappeared under the safe door.

Calling for Blossom to help, I started to move the loose rubble aside so that I could get my fingers under the door. "Right, on three, lift. One, two, three," I ordered. Between us we were able to push the door to one side, only to find a solid oak door underneath the first. Together we lifted this just high enough to see the body of a young woman dressed in dark blue overalls. Using part of the remains of the wooden counter, we managed to wedge the door up so that we could get at the woman. Gently we moved away the bricks and plaster but the more we did so, the more we realised just how badly injured our prisoner was.

"I'll stay here with her, Blossom. You go to the car and call for an ambulance and the fire brigade."

Our prisoner lost consciousness almost as soon as Blossom had gone, and I was left to try and work out what to do for the best. It was obvious the woman had been standing outside the office door when the safe had been blown. It was equally obvious that they had used too much explosive, which had blown the safe door across the room. It and the blast had hit the oak door and torn it from its hinges, and both doors had collapsed on top of our prisoner. Even though Blossom and I had lifted the doors, one leg was still trapped near the ankle under them.

As I shone the torch around my immediate area, I suddenly noticed there was a large dark wet stain getting steadily larger on and around the knee area of the trapped left leg. Gently I touched the wet and immediately could feel the pulsing of blood being pumped from inside the material. There could be no doubt the artery was severed, more than likely by a part of the fractured femur. There was no time to lose: I must find the pressure point and stop the bleeding or she would die. I knew that it would be useless trying to arrange to do it through the overalls, I must get to the bare flesh.

After dealing with a rash of suicides in recent months, I had taken to carrying a pocket knife with me, one which I kept razor sharp after having to use it rather like a saw to cut down a man who would have hanged himself had we not arrived just in time to save him. Hastily I took the knife from my pocket and slit open the leg of the overalls and then the leg of the slacks she was wearing underneath. The spurting blood became evident as the clothing was cut away but it was obvious from how little there was that she was in a very serious condition. I slipped my two hands up her thigh and located the indentation in her groin and pressed hard, one thumb on top of the other. Within seconds the spurting stopped and I hoped that it was because of my pressure and not because there was no more to come. I looked hard at her face. The lips were pale and her eyes were closed, but I could just make out that she was in fact breathing. It was then that I recognised her face. It was Sandy, the girl from Bic's Coffee Bar. "Well I'll be..." I said out loud.

"You'll be arrested if you keep your hands up there, you dirty b–," came Blossom's voice from somewhere behind a torch-beam. "I can't leave you for two minutes without your molesting the birds, can I?" he continued. "What's on then, Dick?"

"She's severed her femoral artery, I think. I just managed to get to the pressure point in time," I replied.

"You stay there, my dear, the fire boys and the ambulance are on the way. By the way, the one out front is female as well. All her face is cut up bad, but I would say she's a youngster," Blossom told me.

"If she's who I think she is, then she claims to be seventeen but she looks about fourteen. How the hell they found out how to do this kind of caper I don't know, but it's a pity they had to learn the hard way how much of the stuff to use."

With the aid of the fire brigade and the ambulance men, both girls were taken to hospital and after quite a long time, they were fit enough to be charged. They admitted that they had committed all the "blowings" and had learnt how to do it when they had discovered a book issued to their father during the war when he was in the Sappers. The explosives had been obtained by swapping their "services" for sticks of gelignite from a Kent coal-miner who came home to visit his widowed mother; she just happened to live next door to the sisters who were aged sixteen and seventeen and a half respectively. As they said, "Who would suspect two girls with a make-up bag?" Which all goes to prove that the criminal does not have to be male; wear black trousers; a striped shirt and a mask, and carry a big black bag marked "Swag".

CHAPTER 10

Although the war had been over for just about eleven years, housing and overcrowding were two of the major problems of the times. To help ease the situation a little, the post-war Government retained many of the large houses that had been requisitioned during the war for military purposes. These were divided into bed-sitters, two-roomed flats for couples with children and even three rooms for the more energetic couples with several children. These houses were known as half-way houses. Families did not stay in them for too long and from there would be allocated a Council house or flat. Despite all the care and attention taken by the local authority who ran them, there were inevitably disputes between the families. These were over the noise of the children or over the use of the one bathroom and toilet shared by as many as three or four families at any one time. Slowly, many of the houses which were in a very bad state of repair were emptied and returned to the pre-war owners or their descendants. By this time, the once beautiful and grand old houses were no longer habitable by their original owners. They stood empty for years, the target for vagrants, thieves and vandals whilst the owners attempted to get just compensation from the Government.

The first in our area to become completely empty was Buckland House. It had been the home of many distinguished people since it was originally built in 1765. Most of the owners had added to or altered the premises and the result resembled a house which had been built by a disagreeing committee. By far its most beautiful feature had been its garden; in spite of the military occupation, when the only things planted in it were staff cars and lorries, the succession of children who had desecrated all living things to a height of six feet, and the terrible winter of 1947 when there was a lot of trouble over the occupants chopping up doors and balustrades for burning, most of the magnificent trees had survived. Now the garden was a jungle of weeds capable of hiding any thief, who only had to duck down to be completely hidden. Whenever I was posted to six beat I always made a point of visiting Buckland House before and after refreshment, mainly because on my very first visit to the house I had arrested two teenagers for stealing parts of the lead plumbing.

One warm, mid-summer evening, the setting sun was turning the giant cedar trees a fiery red as I strolled across what had once been the croquet lawn to the rear door of the west wing of the ramshackle old house. As I reached the door, which was hanging by one hinge at a very strange angle, I turned and tried to imagine what it must have been like a hundred years ago, long before the mass called London had gobbled up the fields which for so many centuries had supplied all that the house had needed to survive. I was just about to light up a cigarette when I heard a noise from inside the house. Slowly and carefully I entered the hallway and stood and listened. There it came again, the sound of quiet and careful footsteps of at least two people, one lighter than the other. Should I go in after them or call for assistance? There was a telephone box not two hundred yards down the road. Discretion being the better part of valour, and the fact that only two weeks ago PC Tony Yorke had been set upon by someone armed with a piece of four-by-two wood, made me decide to telephone for assistance. I crept out of the house and walked carefully along the side wall until I was out of sight of the west-wing windows. Then I trotted out into the road and to the telephone box. Ring ring, ring ring, "Emergency. Which service do you require?" came the voice of the operator.

"Police, New Scotland Yard, please. The number I am speaking from is Ryford 2454," I replied in correct training-school manner.

"Thank you, hold the line please, I'm connecting you."

Ring ring, ring ring. "Police, New Scotland Yard, can I help you?"

"This is PC 1234 attached to Ryford. Buckland Park Road, junction of Cedar Road, meet PC re suspects on premises in empty house. A dog would be a great help as the premises are very large."

"Right, hold the line." Within a minute the operator came back. "Oscar 6 have a dog on board and should be with you in approximately seven minutes."

"Thanks very much." I replaced the receiver and made my way back to the junction, hoping that the suspects would not be gone when we got there.

The wireless car glided gently to a halt beside me. The driver was "Blossom" Trevellyn, with Tony Yorke as his wireless operator. In the back was my old friend, Teddy, with his handler, Harry Sanderson. "What you got then, Dick?" Blossom enquired.

"I've just been round to Buckland House and I can hear someone in there. There are two of them, I think," I replied.

"OK,"said Harry."Blossom and Tony position yourselves in the garden so that you can snap anyone we flush out. Dick, you show me where you last heard them. Come on, Teddy, let's see what we can find." I led the way into the garden and Blossom and Tony left us to take up their positions.

"It's just round here, Harry," I said, as we turned the corner at the end of the west wing. As I spoke a youth of about 18 jumped out of a ground floor window into the garden not 10 yards in front of us. Before we could say or do anything, he put both hands above his head and started to walk towards us.

"All right mate, I give up. I ain't runnin' if you've got 'im 'ere," he said, indicating Teddy. Teddy stopped dead in his tracks and looked at the youth then round at Harry Sanderson, then back to the youth again.

"Stand still, and don't move," Harry ordered. The youth stopped immediately and Teddy walked slowly forward and stopped in front of him.

"Where's the gear you've nicked?" I demanded.

"In the grass under the winder." The youth replied sullenly.

I went to retrieve it but could hardly lift it. "Full to the brim with bluey, Harry," I reported.

"Right, where's your mate? Is he still in there?"

"I don't know what yer talkin' about. There's only me. There ain't no-one else. Look, I got this gear out of the basement. I was just startin' on fillin' me another bag when I 'ears these noises from upstairs so, thinkin' it was you lot, I decided to get out before you come down and find me."

"What do you think, Dick?" asked Harry Sanderson.

"Well, there was definitely two people walking about upstairs," I said.

"All right then, here's what we'll do. We'll hand chummy over to Blossom while you, me and Teddy find his mate."

"I told you, I ain't got no mate. I'm by meself," protested the youth.

I signalled Blossom, who came over to us. "Look after chummy here. We're going to have a look inside," said Harry. "Right, Teddy." Teddy looked up at him expectantly and as Harry took a step forward, Teddy walked up to the youth, sniffed his trousers, turned, lifted his hind leg and sprayed all down the youth's right leg. "Go and find them," ordered Harry.

At this the dog took off down the hallway. As it got to each room, it entered, sniffed at all the cupboards and moved on to the next room. The ground floor completed, he started up the stairs. When he reached the small landing half-way up, he stopped and growled quietly. "Stay, Teddy. You got a torch with you, Dick?" I nodded. "Right. When he finds something, we'll put our torches on together, OK?"

"OK, Harry. What's that?"

From somewhere above us came the rhythmic sound of something being moved backwards and forwards in a sawing motion. Mixed with it were a few muffled gurgles and squeaks.

"Right. When I send him off, we follow as fast as we can. Get him, Teddy."

At the command, Teddy charged up the stairs and along the landing and stopped at a closed door, growling. When we reached the door there could be no doubt that this was where the noises were coming from. "I'll open the door for him and we'll go in right on his tail, torches blazing," ordered Harry. So saying, he slowly turned the handle and threw the door wide open. In rushed Teddy, with both of us immediately behind him. By the light of our torches we saw a man and a woman lying on an old mattress stark naked (except that the man was still wearing his socks – I wonder why they always leave their socks on) and apparently so far gone that our sudden entry into the room went unnoticed. They just went right on with what they were doing.

Teddy looked at the illuminated scene, took two steps forward and sank his teeth into the couple's now fast-moving, rounded flesh. The house shook as screams of terrible, sudden agony echoed round it, rising to a higher pitch as they took on a note of ecstasy before subsiding into sobs of pain. Teddy released his hold, returned to Harry and sat beside him with what could only be described as a very satisfied grin on his face.

Blood was everywhere. I ran to the window and called out for Tony Yorke to get the first-aid kit from the car and to call for an ambulance. Whilst we waited for Tony to arrive, we tried our best to stop the bleeding, using some of the couple's clothing. Tony came through the door with the first-aid kit and his torch blazing, to see Harry Sanderson dabbing at a man's bare rear end with a pair of underpants while I had my arm around a naked woman and was trying to pull her up into a sitting position. When the ambulance arrived there was even more confusion. The two casualties refused to go in the same ambulance or to the same hospital. It turned out that the man was married to the woman's sister and that the woman was also married. The problem was solved only when the ambulance crew called for a second ambulance, which took the woman to another hospital. I have often wondered how they explained away their injuries to their families. As for Teddy, "I suppose this means he'll want rump steak for his grub for a week now," sighed Harry Sanderson.

That draughty, damp old house would have made a chilly meeting-place for lovers except in the heat of summer. In fact, the weather is an all-important factor in the type of incidents that police officers have to contend with. For example, it is a proven fact that there are far fewer suicides in the good summer months than there are in the cold damp days of winter. Also, the types of offences committed are seasonal. For obvious reasons there are very few indecent exposures (flashers) in six inches of snow and temperatures below zero, although I do remember one who claimed that the cold heightened his sexual desires. Having seen the colour of him when he was eventually arrested, I am sure that he was auditioning for the part of the fourth wise monkey. Strangely, the only two women flashers I ever dealt with both occurred in winter when there was snow on the ground.

However, that summer seemed to be one long heatwave. Towards the end of it I was posted early turn on the wireless car with Ted Brewer. Apart from playing drums in our impromptu pop group at Davis's music shop, Ted's main claim to fame was as Ryford nick's local Casanova. About 35 years old, six feet tall, balding, in good condition physically, Ted considered himself God's answer to all women. It was his proud boast that he once struck lucky with the Mother Superior who was the matron of the local children's home. Just how true this was no one really knew, but there was no doubt that they always greeted one another in a very familiar way. As far as is known, no one could pluck up courage to ask her, either.

The very first time I had been out with Ted as observer on the wireless car of which he was the driver, we had received a call at about 8 o'clock in the evening: "Papa 26, Papa 26. 127 Station Approach, Ryford. Believed person of unsound mind. Ends, origin, MP1742." Ted had turned the car into Station Road and pulled up outside number 127, a normal suburban semi, three-bedroomed house, with a small but neat front garden, a ten-year-old car in the drive and a big black cat sitting on the doorstep. Ted reached forward and pushed the door bell, but as he did so the front door was flung wide open. There, framed in the doorway, was a gorgeous ash-blonde in her late twenties, dressed in a pair of fur-trimmed slippers and a very brief housecoat. Ted took one look then he pulled his stomach in, preened himself, took off his cap, brushed his sparse hair with his free hand and said, "You called for the police, my dear?"

"Yes! Yes! Do come in, officers," she said hurriedly, in a voice which was full of eastern promise and fully in keeping with her looks. As we entered the house, Ted's arm gently resting on her shoulder, she burst into tears.

"Now, now, my dear, what's it all about?" asked Ted.

"It's my husband, he's over-sexed," she sobbed.

It was then that I noticed that Ted's neck appeared to be redder than when we entered the house. Ted placed his hat on the hall table and said in a quiet, reassuring voice, "Come now, my dear, what makes you say that?"

"He wants it at least twice a day and is always very forceful. I want to be loved tenderly."

The reddening was now up to Ted's ears. I was completely lost with this one, which was well out of my experience. Let the expert get on with it, I thought. Stand back, watch and learn.

"It does sound to be rather excessive," agreed Ted, "but it certainly isn't that unusual."

Not unusual! I should be half so lucky! Never mind that, concentrate on what she's saying and stop using your imagination, I said to myself. Suddenly I was jolted out of my thoughts as I heard the woman say, "Not excessive? Look what he did to me ten minutes ago." At the same time she threw open her housecoat to reveal a baby doll nightdress which had been ripped right down the front. This in turn showed nothing but a beautiful suntan with no white marks. The whole of Ted's head was now red, but it was nothing to

what it was ten seconds later when she took hold of both his hands saying, "What's more, he keeps on kneading my breasts. Like this, officer." At the same time she placed his hands on her ample breasts and began to rotate them slowly. "Like this, officer," she said again. I swear that there was steam coming out of Ted's ears and that he was so red that he could easily have been mistaken for a pillar-box. From then on, Ted took no active part in the proceedings.

Just at that moment, the door opened from the sitting room and there stood six feet two inches of muscle. Luckily he stood with his head bowed, muttering that he was ashamed of himself and that he would be more considerate in future. I advised the lady as to her civil rights should these promises not be fulfilled and then it was time to leave. I picked up Ted's hat, placed it on his head and steered the glazed-eyed driver back to the wireless car.

The report had to be as full as possible to avoid any future complications should a complaint be made at a later date. However, Ted was never quite the same after that evening. My wife had a lot of innocent pleasure waiting for Ted to be posted to a foot patrol, then walking up behind him and saying, "Like this, officer." Her delight came as the red crept up over his face, especially when she asked, "Was she a true ash-blonde, officer?"

On the occasion that summer when I was on early turn with Ted, we left the station after our refreshments at about 10.45 am and already the temperature was well into the eighties. "There's not much point in driving around in this heat, Dick. We'll go over to Axehurst Common and sit up in the shade in one of the car parks. OK?"

"Whatever you say, Ted. It's too bloody hot to do anything."

We had only been sitting for about fifteen minutes, doors open, jackets undone and caps off, when the radio spluttered into life: "27 Blackdown Road, see informant, indecent exposure." I acknowledged the message and we set off for the scene of the call. It was not too far and we were there within five minutes. As we neared the address we slowed so that we could check for any likely suspects but there was no one to be seen in the immediate vicinity. We pulled up outside the address and I went to the front door and rang the bell. Ted stood just inside the front gate. The door opened and there stood a good-looking woman, aged about thirty-five and dressed in a two-piece bathing costume.

Before I could say anything, I was pushed to one side as ladykiller Ted Brewer went into action. His well-tried and perfected approach was as smooth as silk. It would have left Don Juan speechless. It was the master at work and I could only watch in amazed admiration. How he did it I still don't know and I was standing beside him, but within half a minute he had his arm around the woman's shoulders with her crying into his chest. "There, there, my dear. Don't distress yourself, he's gone now. Let's go indoors so that you can sit down and compose yourself." As he was saying this, he was trying to indicate to me to go back to the car and wait. I had just made up my mind to go when another woman aged about sixty appeared in the doorway, obviously the informant's mother. Completely unaffected by her arrival on the scene, Ted continued holding the informant and at the same time started chatting up the mother. Within seconds she was simpering at him as well. I just stood, mouth slightly open, staring in disbelief. There could be no doubt at all that what was said at Ryford station about no female between sixteen and sixty being safe if Ted was about was true. As I stood there, I wondered to myself what he had got that I couldn't get cured, even if it was younger than his. Strangely, in all the years I served with Ted, I never once knew of a complaint being made by any woman or husband about him. He once confided to me that he had a rota system with about seven of his regulars. His wife Angela, typical of her superior attitude, seemed to deliberately ignore his extra curricular activities, and in the realms of stamina he was a better man than I could ever dream of being.

"I was pegging out the washing on the line in the back garden when I heard a man's voice say, "What do you think of this then, darling?" I looked about and could not see anyone. Then after about thirty seconds, I heard his voice again, asking the same question. As I expect you know, there's a public footpath which runs between the bottom of the gardens to these houses and the recreation ground. All the houses are fenced off from the footpath by a six-foot close-board fence. Well, as I continued to hang out my washing, this man's voice kept asking the same question and it was getting louder. I had got over half-way down the garden when I noticed a man's penis sticking through the knot-hole in the fence at the bottom of the garden. Every so often it disappeared, all was quiet and then it would appear again and the man called out. I can only think that he peered through the hole every so often to make certain that I was there."

"What did you do?" asked Ted in a gentle soothing voice.

"I continued hanging out my washing, working down the garden path and getting nearer to him. My husband has been rough-digging a patch of ground at the bottom of the garden and his spade was still stuck in the earth. When I got to within reach of it, I pulled it out of the ground, swung it over my shoulder and hit his penis end on with the flat blade of the spade."

At this statement I involuntarily flinched and took a quick breath. For his part, Ted paled slightly and asked, "What happened then?"

"The man screamed and I ran indoors and telephoned you."

Needless to say, there was no description available of the suspect, except that he would have a mushroom-shaped appendage. Somehow I did not feel that we could justifiably stop every man in a three-mile radius and ask to be allowed to make an examination without getting arrested ourselves. It was in the casualty department of Ryford General Hospital that we eventually found our man. He was trying to explain what had happened to him. We charged him two weeks later, after he had been released from hospital. When he appeared in court, the Chairman of the Magistrates had difficulty in keeping a straight face when the details were outlined to the court after "Shorty" (as his mates at work had nicknamed him) had pleaded guilty. The Chairman took the only possible action – he bound him over to keep the peace!

The next day was even hotter. Ted had found a coolish spot underneath the beech trees in the driveway which led to Ryford golf course. This was an eighteen-hole championship course and was regarded as being the top one in many a square mile. "We won't be able to stay here long," muttered Ted.

"Why not?" I asked. "It's about the coolest place we've found all day."

"I agree, but I happen to know that the District Commander, Mad Dave Radler plays a round of golf here every Thursday afternoon. We'd better not be sitting here when he comes."

"Ok, let's have a slow spin around the ground, then we'll go to one of the car parks on Axehurst Common."

Ted started up the car and we turned out of the driveway just as Mad Dave Radler turned into it. "Told you so," said Ted, and we made our way by a roundabout route to Axehurst Common.

"Thank God you've come in here. Please help me. He's dead. I don't know what to do," exclaimed a woman in her late forties as she came running across the gravel of Axehurst Common's little car park.

Ted slammed on the brakes and the car stopped with a jolt. Before he could switch off, I was out of the car and just managed to catch the woman as she started to slump on the ground. I propped her against the boot of the wireless car and fanned her with a newspaper.

When she came round, she was able to tell us what was wrong. Her voice was very low and her head was bowed, but we were able to piece together the story. "That's my car parked over there and beside it is my next-door neighbour's car," she said, pointing to the only other two cars in the car park. "We both live in Epsom. We've been having an affair for many months now and we regularly meet in isolated car parks well away from home so that his wife and my husband don't find out. Today we met here and were courting in the back seat of my car. We were both very excited and one thing led to another and before long we were having sex. Suddenly he gave a little cry, clutched his chest and went all limp. It has taken me nearly ten minutes to get out from under him, but I can't move him or anything. Can you help me, please? I honestly thought that he was coming, but he went instead."

After reassuring the woman and relating the story to Ted while

trying to keep a straight face, I went over to the woman's car and there, jammed between the back of the front seat and the front of the back seat, was the body of a trouserless man. After a great deal of pulling and pushing we managed to get him out of the car, dressed and into the driving seat of his own car. We then sent the woman on her way home. Later, we put together a report which said that we had been patrolling and had entered the car park, where we had found a man slumped over the steering wheel of his car. We deduced that he had felt ill whilst driving and had pulled into the car park to rest. There he had died. Never let it be said that the police in those days were not compassionate!

CHAPTER 11

"Hey, Dick, are you on seven and eight?" called a voice from the communications room.

"Yes, what have you got? I don't mind what it is so long as it's in the cool somewhere," I replied as I entered the room.

"The Kent Constabulary want two witness statements taken. Here's the message."

I took the copy of the teleprinter message from the reserve man. It read: "Please allow an officer to call on Mr Stanley Michael John Anderson and Mrs Anna Beth Anderson of Sunset House, Blackthorn Lane, Ryford and obtain statements from them both concerning a Personal Injury Road Traffic Accident which they witnessed on ...." I took copies of the appropriate forms and set off to walk the three miles to Blackthorn Lane.

Although the sun was low in the sky, it was still boiling hot. It was going to be a sleepless night for me and many others tonight. As I reached the entrance to Blackthorn Lane, I realised that it was not going to be too difficult to locate the Andersons' house. There on a small hill stood a large, detached, Tudor-style house, bathed in the evening sunlight. Never has a house been more aptly named. Slowly I made my way up Blackthorn Lane until I found a pair of very large and imposing wrought-iron gates. I pushed my way through them and crunched up the long gravel drive which led to a large circular lawn in front of the house. Here the drive divided left and right; the left-hand drive splitting to the front and rear of the house. The huge iron-studded door was closed but there was a wrought-iron bell pull hanging down the wall on the right-hand side of the door. I pulled it and heard the distant sound of a bell ringing somewhere in the house, then turned and gazed out over Ryford. By shading my eyes against the glare of the sun, I was just able to make out Ryford railway station sidings, which managed to keep me awake so well during the day when I was on night duty. I had just started to try to pinpoint other landmarks when I heard the door open behind me. I turned and could just make out a man's face peering round the door. "Mr Anderson? Mr Stanley Michael John Anderson?" I enquired.

"Yes. Can I help you, officer?" came the reply.

"Yes, if you would, sir. You witnessed an accident in Kent two weeks ago, and the Kent Constabulary would like me to take a statement from you and your wife if it is convenient."

"Certainly. Do please come in." With this, he opened the door just enough for me to enter.

As my eyes became accustomed to the inside light, I made out a spacious hallway with black and white floor tiles. It was pleasantly cool after the glare outside. When I was able to distinguish Mr Anderson, who was now standing with his back to the closed door, I was unable to believe my eyes. There stood a good-looking man, aged about thirty to thirty-five, five feet eight inches in height, and absolutely stark naked. I instinctively backed to the wall.

"I do hope you're not embarrassed, officer," said Mr Anderson. "You see, my wife and I are naturists, and we only put on clothes when it is absolutely necessary, especially on a day like this. That's why we bought this house."

"That's all right, sir. I was in the forces and we got used to seeing many strange sights in the billets. If you don't mind, I don't."

"Oh good. You must be sweltering in that uniform. Will you need a table to rest your papers on?"

"Yes, please, if possible, sir. It makes things easier," I replied.

"We had better use the desk in the study, then. Follow me." He strode off down the hall and I followed at a discreet distance, just in case he saw a pin on the floor and bent down to pick it up before I could come to a halt. "Do go in and sit down officer. I'll call my wife. I won't be a moment."

I entered a light, airy room, which had a roll-top desk in the window recess, high-backed, real leather armchairs, a coffee table and other small items of furniture. Above the fireplace was a large painting of a car racing at what appeared to be the old Brooklands

racetrack. I stood admiring this painting with my helmet tucked under my left arm.

"I have just brought us some iced home-made lemonade. I'm sure you could do with one, officer," said a woman's husky and rather sexy voice.

I turned towards the sound and there, entering the room carrying a silver tray with a jug covered by a beaded muslin cloth and three glasses, came a golden pocket Venus. She was beautiful! Aged about twenty-five, five feet two inches tall with waist-length natural ash-blonde hair, there was not one part of her well-proportioned body which was not a golden-brown colour. I stared at her, absorbing every detail. I was only jerked back into reality when I heard my helmet clutter to the floor. "I'm ... I'm very sorry to disturb you both," I stuttered as I bent down to retrieve my helmet. As I started to straighten up, I found my eyes directly in line with the rear of the pocket Venus, who was bending down to place the tray on the coffee table. Somehow the temperature was higher now than it had been all day.

"Would it help if we had an Ordnance Survey map of the area, officer?" asked Mr Anderson.

"Yes, it certainly would, sir," I faltered.

"I think it's in the newspaper rack, darling," said Husky-voice. I'll get it for you." She half-squatted, half-bent over the newspaper rack and for some strange reason my mind flashed to the station cycle-shed.

I took the statements, making them last as long as possible, then stepped out of the house into the late evening light. Strangely, the temperature seemed lower with every step I took away from Sunset House. When I reached the station, I handed the statements and the teleprinter message to the Section Sergeant. He glanced at them and said, "This writing is terrible. Did you dip your tame spider's legs in the ink-pot and let him write it? It's all shaky, Kenyon."

"Yes, Sarge, I know. I'm very sorry about it but I had to write it on a rickety table," I lied. With that I went across the station yard to get my cycle to go home. As I pulled it out of the rack, a smile spread across my face. I hardly slept at all that night it was so hot, and every now and then my imagination made it even hotter.

Perhaps it was just as well that interviewing the Andersons was my last job before my annual leave. My wife, Janet, and I were going away on our very first holiday since we were married. "Is everything in the car?" I shouted to Janet before checking that the taps, electricity and gas were turned off, then slamming the front door behind me.

"It's a good thing we're going to the Romney Marsh," said Janet. "At least it's flat and I won't have to walk up all the hills." Our pride and joy was a 1936 Singer Bantam Saloon which, to say the least, had seen better days. Its complete inability to pull up hills meant that

Janet had to get out and walk up any incline which was more than one in eight. Still, for fifteen pounds, what could one expect?

We eventually arrived at the holiday cottage we had rented for a week. It was one of a pair of semi-detached cottages which were let out during the summer, situated about three miles outside Romney. They were nothing elaborate but had everything we needed, including the garden for the children to play in. We decided that we would spend what was left of the day settling in, and start our trips to the sea and so on the following day.

It must have been all the fresh air but by 9.30 pm we were ready for bed. I locked up and went upstairs with a book on murder, mystery and suspense. Maybe I would learn something. At about 10.30 pm there came the sound of a car pulling up next door. The doors of the car slammed, followed by the boot- lid and the click of the latch of the gate. Next, I heard a woman's voice say, "Oh darling, you are a fool. Mind you don't drop me," immediately followed by giggling. By the sounds that followed, it would have been better if the fellow, whoever he was, had opened the front door first before becoming the gallant. As it was, I got the firm impression that at the very least he had tucked her under his arm and used her head as a battering ram on the front door. Then there was a final crash which sounded as if the last charge of the battering ram had found an open door. They careered headlong down the hallway, eventually ending in a giggling chuckling heap amid the pots and pans in the kitchen. After an hour or so I was just dozing off to sleep when suddenly the room echoed to the sound of a radio being played quite loudly in the bedroom next door. This was accompanied by the occasional noise of what sounded like a bed banging against the wall. Eventually, all was quiet except for the occasional giggle. After what seemed like hours, I eventually went to sleep having put two and two together and arrived at quads.

The next morning the children woke us early. It was a bright, hot, sunny morning and we decided that we would spend the day on the beach. By 9.30 we were ready to leave the house. As we loaded the food and the family into the Singer, I noticed a Rover parked next door. It looked vaguely familiar but I dismissed this from my mind. After all, one pre-war black Rover looked very much like another. We reached the beach and staked out our claim to a nice spot beside a breakwater which sheltered us from the wind. At about midday we realised that we had left the food at the cottage. Rather than lose our spot on the beach, I set off in the car to fetch it, leaving

Janet on the beach with the children. I got to within about half a mile of the cottage when the Singer decided it would help in preparing the lunch by boiling its radiator to make the tea. Leaving it to cool down where it had expired, I walked to the cottage. I went through the front door to the kitchen and collected a basket of food and some water for the car. Whilst filling the bottle, I looked out into the gardens. There to my amazement I saw Shirley Long, who was the fiancée of PC Bill Evans, my colleague at Ryford.

Shirley was one of the most well-endowed young ladies in the whole of Ryford. She was our local Sabrina and Jayne Mansfield all rolled into one. Five feet six inches tall with a 42-26-34 figure and waist-length, wavy red hair styled in a pony-tail, she was the cause of many a turned head as she travelled to and from the Midland Bank where she worked. How or why she had ever fallen for Bill Evans no one would ever know, but you had only to see them together to realise that they were head over heels in love with each other. Strangely, she had had a steadying effect on Bill, and now that they were engaged, his strange pranks had become considerably less. However, from time to time he still could not resist some practical joke to embarrass one of his long-suffering fellow-officers.

I was about to call out to Shirley when her male companion turned so that I could see his face, and I got my second shock: it was Ryford's champion womaniser, Ted Brewer. Now I was as keen as anyone at Ryford nick to see Bill Evans get his come-uppance for all his practical jokes, but this, I thought, was taking it too far – Ted knew that Bill and Shirley had already fixed their wedding date, and he had plenty of other opportunities for indulging in a bit of eider-down-hurdling. Like many of the younger, athletic, good-looking officers, he could afford to pick and choose and still never go hungry. One of the best duties for this sport was school crossings at infant and junior schools, with all the young mums taking their reluctant offspring like lambs to the slaughter every day. It was astonishing just how many officers fall for the lonely housewife routine. Legend has it at Ryford that one officer (not Ted Brewer) was so easily led by these unscrupulous mothers that it was impossible to do a school-crossing duty at any school in Ryford without, sooner or later, coming across a miniature look-alike of this particular officer. I was always very sceptical about this story until one day I was performing school-crossing patrol duties at St Mark's school. It was then that I noticed a rather good-looking, black-haired woman shepherding twin boys with bright red hair and rather large noses

through the school gate. You've guessed it: the officer concerned had bright red hair and a large nose.

Not all these things happen as a result of schools. Police married quarters produce many interesting stories, one of the best of which was about two constables who submitted official reports requesting permission to swap married quarters but the respective wives to remain where they were. The officers used this very complicated approach in an attempt to get official agreement for their wife-swapping. Many police marriages break up under the strain put on wives by the demanding nature of the job and the unsocial hours that policemen have to work, but many break-ups are also due to the husband being unable to resist "a bit on the side". Still, as "Dusty" Miller once confided to me, "For every man who goes astray in the police, there are three or four women who help him, and without them he would be blameless." That may be a rather exaggerated way of trying to excuse infidelities, but it certainly raises a point which is often missed.

As soon as I saw it was Ted Brewer with Shirley in the garden next door, I slipped quietly away, picked up the basket of food and returned to the beach. I naturally told Janet about my discovery, conveniently forgetting to mention that both Ted and Shirley had been wearing the briefest of swimsuits and that Shirley's figure had been a sight worth seeing. After some discussion we decided it was their business and if they wanted to be unfaithful to their partners, then it was up to them. We both felt sorry for Bill Evans, but we would try not to let them see us and would keep very quiet about the whole episode when we returned home. Live and let live.

When we got back to the cottage that evening, the Rover was missing and there was no sign of life next door. After we had eaten and put the children to bed, we sat in the garden enjoying the sunset. We had just decided to go in when we heard the Rover pull up. Quickly we went inside and closed the door, then watched Ted and Shirley walk up the path to the house next door. They were holding hands and talking very earnestly. "You're not mistaken, it is them," said Janet. "In a way I feel sorry for them as well as Bill. They must have planned going away together for some time, only to end up staying next door to someone who could recognise them. It must be called "sod's law" or something."

About an hour later there came the sounds of another car pulling up and its occupants going in next door. Again there were a lot of strange noises and giggles which continued late into the night.

The following morning, there came a knocking at the back door. I opened it and there stood Ted Brewer in pyjamas and dressing gown and holding a small jug. "Good morning. Could you spare us some milk until the shops o.... Good God!!" he exclaimed. Then he turned and ran up the garden path, back to the house next door. I felt sorry for him, but my wife just murmured, "Be sure your sins will find you out."

We got ready to go out for the day and were packing things into the car when I noticed a Hillman Minx parked immediately behind the Rover. Whoever it was who had turned up next door late yesterday had stayed the night. We set off and spent the day on the Hythe canal.

Not long after we had put the children to bed, there came another knocking on the back door. I opened it and there stood Ted Brewer again, but this time he was holding a glass half-full of beer. "Hi there, Dick," he greeted me, obviously trying to keep a straight face. "Shirley and I thought that as you had discovered our secret, you and Janet might like to come round for a drink. You'll be able to hear the kids if they cry. It's no use us hiding now, is it?"

"Come in a minute, Ted. I'll see what Janet says," I replied in a rather surprised voice.

Eventually we agreed to join them as soon as the children were well asleep. Ted went back next door and about ten minutes later we followed him. We knocked on the door and Ted opened it. "Come on in. I think you know us all," he said.

We entered the sitting room to the chorus of "Surprise, surprise!" There we found not only Shirley but Bill Evans and Ted's wife, Angela. Janet and I just stood there, mouths open wide.

"We're sorry but we just couldn't resist the temptation of teasing you when we found out you had rented next door for a week," explained Bill Evans between laughs. "You see, Angie and I are brother and sister. About two years ago our grandmother died and left us this pair of cottages. We decided to do them up, keep one just for our own use and rent out the other as a holiday cottage. When we received your booking, we decided to set it up so that first of all you believed Ted and Shirley were having an affair, and then we were into wife-swapping. By the look on your faces, we succeeded." With this, they all collapsed with laughter.

Janet and I had been well and truly tricked but the only response I could think of was, "I wouldn't have thought an ugly bloke like Bill could have a sister as good-looking as Angela." We sat down and Ted poured us some beer. "One of these days, Bill," I added, "one of these days I'll get even with you."

CHAPTER 12

I stood transfixed by the beauty of it all. I felt as if I were the centre pillar of a pair of very old pan-scales, just like those depicted as being held by the blindfold "Justice". In one pan was the golden, throbbing, vibrant orb of the setting sun, its light filling the whole of the western sky and turning the few wisps of cloud into golden leaves, and in the other pan was the huge, rose-tinted marble face of the man in the harvest moon. It filled the eastern horizon, slowly revealing more of itself. I wondered whether, if I stood on tiptoe, I could create hand-shadow images on the face of the moon. It is moments like this that make the freezing rains of winter worth enduring as a necessary evil to enable us to pass through another year waiting for the beauty of these few minutes.

Slowly the balance tilted, the sun getting lower and its rays turning the side of the hill to red with lengthening black shadows. Suddenly the tranquillity of it all was shattered by the piercing screams of a child in terror and extreme pain. They came from below me, from the woods at the bottom of the hill. So deeply engrossed with the natural beauty of the scene had I been that I literally jumped with surprise. In an instant I started to run down the hill in the direction of the screams. Now the sight of a policeman, running in full uniform, is laughable in itself; heavy boots, uniform and a helmet are not exactly the right dress for either sprinting or marathon running. But add to this the fact that I was running down a one-in-five grass slope towards a line of trees four hundred yards away with the whole scene being performed in a sea of red, then one has a possible opening scene of the descent into Dante's Inferno.

As I half ran and half fell down the hill, I constantly changed direction in an effort to home in on the screams. I burst into the trees and descended about another fifty yards, catching hold of the trunks of trees with either hand where I could, in an effort to check my headlong plunge down the hill. Suddenly I found myself on the edge of a small clearing and the sight that greeted me was, to say the least, not pleasant. There, in the centre of the clearing, was a small boy aged about two or three. His right wrist and hand were gripped in the mouth of an amber-eyed, almost black Alsatian dog, whilst his left leg was in the jaws of an almost identical dog. On the edge of the clearing cowered a young woman, rigid with fright. Her mouth was wide open but no sound came from it. Hardly checking my pace, I drew my truncheon and lashed out at the nearest dog. I felt the blow strike home on its shoulder. The dog yelped and released its hold. I slithered by and frantically tried to reverse my direction to attack the second dog. Before I managed to get within striking distance, it released its hold and the pair snarled their way out of the clearing. This was my first encounter with what was known locally as "The Hounds of Axehurst".

Briefly, the story of this poor child was that he and his mother were having a picnic when the two dogs came up to them. The dogs advanced, ears laid back and snarling, and attempted to take some of the food. The woman had tried to shoo the dogs away and her son had copied her, whilst still holding a sandwich in his right hand. One of the dogs grabbed at the sandwich but the child clung to it. In the struggle that immediately followed, the second dog also attacked, the hunting instinct of the dog being to assist the other member of the pack with the "kill".

This was just another incident in a catalogue of events for which a small pack of wild Alsatians had been responsible over the past eighteen months. It was believed that a stray bitch had teamed up with a male dog and the pack consisted of them and a litter of puppies which were now full-grown. They had survived by reverting to their natural instinct, killing rabbits, birds and other animals, and scavenging. About five months previously, the bitch and a litter of week-old puppies had been caught in a fox hole. This left the old male dog and three full-grown youngsters. These had been reduced to two by the attentions of a shepherd protecting his lambs with a shotgun. The two I had encountered were the old dog and his son.

As it turned out, this was not to be my only encounter with "The Hounds of Axehurst". It was mid-November and although it was only five o'clock in the evening, already the fog was beginning to close in. Hopefully it would not be too thick tonight. I entered Ryford nick front office to book in for my refreshments.

"Ah, the very man," said Sergeant Tom Price, the station officer, in response to my "All correct, Sergeant" report. "It is you who wants to become a dog-handler, isn't it?"

My heart leaped. It had come, the moment I had been waiting for, there was a vacancy and the Sergeant was going to tell me to put in an application. My excitement was dashed instantly when Tom Price said, "Well, this is right up your street. It'll give you the necessary experience and must help you when you apply for a vacancy. I've just had a request from the station officer at Axehurst for a van and one officer to assist the RSPCA Inspector to catch the "Hounds of Axehurst" which are cornered in a shed."

"Thanks very much, Sergeant. I've already had a run-in with them," I said in a voice heavy with wasted sarcasm.

"What better?" came his instant reply. "You know what you're dealing with. In a job like this experience is everything. Go and dig out Angus, he's van driver, and get off right away. You can eat your grub on the way." So saying, he returned his attention to the typewriter which was in danger of bursting into flames at any second with the speed it was being used at. "Sergeant Tom Price joined the force to catch criminals, not to be a bloody typist – that's what my daughter is training to be:" that was what he told anyone who mentioned his typing. Since he had been promoted four years earlier, he had made definite progress. Now, although still searching the keyboard for the right letter with the index finger poised, ready to stab the key, he did have the index fingers of both hands poised, something like a praying mantis. When the correct key was located, the finger struck with all the speed of a paralysed cobra. Police typing pools were years away.

PC Angus Macleod, Class 1 Police Driver, master of speed on two, three or four wheels, sat with a resigned look on his face as the Morris Commercial van laboured its way up Axehurst Water Tower hill. Whenever he was posted van driver, Angus became very downcast and the three weeks posting always proved to be hell for his family. It wasn't his fault that he loved speed – speed was the thing which kept Angus alive. He had a deep need for it, almost like a drug addict for cocaine.

"We're to go to Axehurst and pick up the RSPCA Inspector, who knows where to go," I mumbled between mouthfuls of corned-beef sandwich.

"I ken where to go right enough, as far awa' as possible from yon dogs. I'm just the driver. You'll have to deal wi' the dogs, understand?" snapped Angus.

"All right, all right, I understand," I muttered as the van crested the top of the hill and accelerated slowly over the next mile and a half before reaching its top speed of 45 mph, flat out, downhill with a strong following wind. Eventually we arrived at Axehurst nick where we found the RSPCA Inspector waiting for us outside the front door. As we pulled up he jumped on board and gave Angus directions to some allotment gardens about two miles away.

Senior Inspector Eric Black was a man of vast experience and was regarded as being the Royal Society for the Prevention of Cruelty to Animals top man in the area. Eric explained that several of the local people had succeeded in trapping the two Alsatians by placing a bitch on heat in a partitioned area in the back of one of the sheds. They had lain in hiding until the dogs had entered the shed and then slammed the door shut on them. We were able to get the van to within 20 yards of the shed. As we pulled up we could hear the dogs desperately trying to escape by throwing themselves at the door, gnawing and scratching at the bottom of it whilst all the time howling and snarling. Eric and I got out of the van carrying two misnamed "dog catchers" which were carried as part of the standard equipment of the van.

Dog catchers were remarkably simple in their construction and in the theory of their use. A length of sash cord about six feet long was fastened by means of a knot into a metal block which, in turn, was welded to a thick-walled iron pipe about an inch in diameter and three feet long. The sash cord passed up through the pipe with a knot tied in the other end to stop it being pulled back through the pipe. The operator made a loop in the cord at the bottom, large enough for a dog's head to pass through, placed it over the dog's head, quickly pulled up the slack rope at the top and wrapped it round his hand; the dog was then restrained and capable of being managed. These pieces of equipment were great in theory but obviously designed by someone who had never attempted to catch a dog in his life. They had many drawbacks, the biggest of which was their restricted use in a confined space. It was obvious from the size of the shed that they could not be used in this situation.

"You stay outside, ready with the catcher, and I'll see if I can get them to eat some of these tranquillising tablets," said Eric Black, showing me a handful of yellow tablets. "Be very quiet but be ready to come instantly if I shout for you." So saying, he slowly opened the shed door a fraction. As the door was unlatched, one of the dogs hurled itself at it. Such was the force, he was able to slide through the gap and escape. There was a faint curse from Eric but he continued into the shed, closing the door behind him.

The noises inside, a mixture of snarls, growls, barking and whimpering, plus the quiet and steady voice of Eric talking, lasted for nearly three-quarters of an hour, then the door opened slowly. "Catcher, noose first, as fast as you can, Dick," said Eric quietly. I hastily passed in the catcher. "Take the slack in, he's all yours. Watch him," came the relieved voice of Eric.

I did as I was told and pulled on the pipe and managed to drag the still struggling Alsatian from the shed. Whilst he was in there, Eric had used his neck-tie as a muzzle around the dog's mouth to save himself being bitten. "He should be out cold, the number of tablets I've stuffed down him, but they don't appear to be slowing him down at all," said Eric.

We took the dog to the van which was now parked over a hundred yards away, Angus having decided that the vicinity of the shed and biting dogs were no place for him. "That's the old one we've caught," Eric told me. "I think we'll wait and see if the youngster comes back. I've put some food in there laced with crushed tablets. After all, a youngster is far more likely to chance his all for love than an old dog who knows the truth of the saying, another day, another way." So we settled down and waited. After about half an hour, the young dog slipped back into the shed. We did not rush to lock him in but waited another half-hour before Eric, armed with the second catcher, slowly entered the shed.

The inside of a Morris Commercial police van held the basic needs that the various uses it was put to demanded. Behind the driver was a partition which extended across the van to the centre. Down both sides of the van were long bench seats which had lockers under them. The lockers contained all manner of goodies: a stretcher; rubber sheet for dead bodies; tow rope; dog catchers; first aid kit; various tools; in fact anything which could be useful. There was an official list of items to be carried but these had been added to, to cover local requirements. Beside the driver was a separate passenger seat which faced forward, and in the narrow gangway between the bench seats, lying on the metal floor, was a long metal ramp used for getting police Velocette motorcycles to the district garage for repair, or recovering lost or stolen motorcycles. This contraption was responsible for more twisted ankles than the miles of pavement which were walked every day. The gap down the centre was so small that if you sat opposite someone your knees had to interlace with theirs. It was into this space that Eric Black and I manoeuvred our struggling prisoners.

Eric went in first and braced himself in the corner against the partition behind Angus, the dog on the floor facing towards the double rear doors. I slid in and wedged myself into the corner at the rear made by the bolted door and the nearside of the van, each of us placing a foot on a dog's neck in an attempt to further restrain them. Angus slammed the rear doors closed by pushing them with his outstretched hands. When they closed he came forward and ensured they were fastened, then he went to the driver's door which was closed. "Are ye sure yon beasties are held safe?" he shouted. We assured him that they were and slowly he slid the door open and climbed inside. "Where are we taking 'em, then?" he enquired.

"We could never leave them in a police station yard, they'll have to go direct to Battersea Dogs' Home," replied Eric Black.

Muttering to himself, Angus started the van and reluctantly, and with obvious apprehension, started the 20-mile journey to Battersea. The fog had held off and there was only a mist which was just thick enough to slow the traffic without bringing it to a standstill. Slowly we picked our way through south London, with Angus spending as much time looking over left shoulder to make sure that we still had control over the dogs, as he did looking forward. By the time we reached New Cross Gate, what little effect the tranquillisers eaten by the old dog had had was wearing off fast. Every minute he became stronger and my battle to keep him on the floor became harder.

As I stared at the dogs on the floor in the small amount of light that came into the van from the street lamps, I became aware that the fingers on my right hand which had the rope wrapped around it were a strange shade of blue. I had no option but to unwrap the rope and try to swap hands. I unwound the rope very carefully, trying to keep the pull on it the whole time. In the split second that the rope was loose, the old dog seized his opportunity and slid out from under my foot with the now slack noose and pipe hanging from his neck. In what was apparently one movement he tore a large lump out of the left leg of my trousers as he came up from the floor, heading directly for my face and throat. I shouted a warning and instinctively put up my hands to protect myself. The next 30 seconds were a complete chaos and what exactly happened is uncertain. However, what is certain is that Eric Black, whilst still trying to restrain his dog, managed to drag the old dog away from my throat. I regained hold of the catcher and tightened the noose and, after a struggle, managed to get the dog back onto the floor of the van.

As things quietened down, I became aware that there was something different. Initially I could not work out what it was, then I realised that the van was not moving. Not only that but we did not have a driver: Angus had gone! There we were, stationary, engine running, in the middle of the northbound lane of the Old Kent Road. "Angus, where the hell are you?" I shouted. No reply. "Angus!" I shouted again.

This time I heard the driver's door slide open a little, a very little. "Have ye catched the bastard animal?"

"Aye, we catched it, ye are safe the noo," Eric mimicked, winking at me. Very carefully Angus eased his way into the driving seat, and with even greater caution, drove on.

"Here we are, then. I'll get them to open the gate so that we can

drive right inside." So saying, Angus was gone.

"I do hope there's someone readily available. The drugs have worn off both dogs now," said Eric. We sat and waited, well over ten minutes we waited, but still no sign of Angus. "Do you think you can manage both of them for a minute whilst I find out what's happening?" asked Eric.

"I'll try," I replied. "Let's get my foot on your dog's neck and then give me your catcher and rope, but hurry up."

So Eric left me in charge of both dogs. "Won't be a minute," he called as he climbed out of the van.

He had been gone about three minutes when Angus returned to the van. "Who's the idiot who left your door open?" he shouted. The next second he slammed the door shut. At the sound of this, both dogs were startled into renewed violent struggles. The young dog managed to pull the rope and the catcher from my left hand whilst the old dog's struggles succeeded in breaking the weld which held the metal block to the pipe of the catcher. This of course meant that he was completely free. The young dog rushed into the driver's compartment but, finding no escape route, swung round and came back. As he did so the catcher swung into the windscreen and smashed it. The old dog came up from the floor like a cork out of a bottle, and again I instinctively pushed out my hands in front of me. This time I found and managed to take hold of the fur on the front of his neck and hold him at arm's length. The two front doors and the rear door were swung open together and Eric Black and two women from the dogs' home managed to catch both dogs and drag them through the gate into the home. I felt exhausted, I was sweating like a pig and my mouth was dry. With shaking hands I managed to roll a resemblance to a cigarette and light it and gratefully accepted the offer of a cup of tea from the dogs' home ladies.

About four months later, I was informed that the Senior Inspector, Eric Black, and I were to receive RSPCA awards in connection with the events of that day. Coincidently, it was on the same day as police wireless car driver Class 1 Angus Macleod became involved in a chase of a bank-raid getaway car at well over 90 mph and eventually arrested a man armed with a sawn-off shotgun. Angus subsequently received the Queen's Commendation for Bravery.

Myself, I have always been very wary of geese.

CHAPTER 13

"Fancy a cuppa, lad?" The invitation came from a wizened old man who looked at least a hundred years old, as he drew himself upright from weeding the flower-bed beside the west door of St George's Church.

"Yes please, Charlie," I replied. "I'll just slip down to the box and make my ring, it's due now. Then I'll be back."

"No rush, lad. I'm not as sprightly as I used to be. It should just about be ready when you get back."

I walked to number two box and made my scheduled ring into Ryford station. This done, I made my way back to St George's Church. "Coming down, Charlie," I called out as I reached the top of the steep steps leading into the church crypt.

Carefully I picked my way down the wet, slippery stone steps. At the bottom I turned sharp right through a small archway and knocked on the thick wooden door. "Come on in, lad," came a faint voice from the room. I opened the door inwards and the bright light of the hundred-watt bulb made me blink. "I used to get quite a few of you lads coming down here once upon a time but now there's only about three of you, two old-timers and you, lad. Take sugar?" the old man asked as he busied himself in the corner.

"Yes, please. Two if you can spare it," I replied.

"If I couldn't spare it, I wouldn't have asked," came the curt reply.

"Sorry," I apologised.

"Take a pew," the old man said, chuckling to himself. "Pew in the boiler- house of a church, get it?" he enquired.

I agreed, giving a rather hollow laugh; after all, it was the same joke every time. It was funny the first time but now, some twenty-plus times on, the humour had gone out of it. I would laugh at anything old Charlie said though to keep myself welcome at this watering-hole. On my very first beat with him, when we had visited the ticket office of Ryford railway station, "Dusty" Miller had taught me the importance of such spots and Charlie's was in the upper bracket of the watering-holes on Ryford's ground.

St George's Church was situated on the corner of the crossroads which marked the meeting-point of the boundaries of four different beats. In summer months, the boiler-house was lovely and cool, situated just off the crypt and deep below the church proper. In the winter, on the night before any service or special occasion, it was beautifully warm. Charlie Knight was a retired police officer who had left the force before I was even born. He eked out his pension by being the part-time caretaker, boilerman and gardener at the church. He, of all people, knew just how valuable a location such as his boiler-room was to the constable on the beat. There was a gas-ring, kettle, tea and teapot, matches, powdered milk, mugs and two armchairs. There was also a wash-basin to wash up the cups. This was one of the watering-holes where, every now and then, the visiting night duty beat-man accidently dropped a quarter-pound packet of tea or a florin, which for some strange reason he could never find.

Every watering-hole has stories associated with it, depending on its location and type. For example, there was the rear room of the newsagent's in East Street where the instant coffee was good, fast, sweet, strong and hot – as was the 25-year-old nymphomaniac who worked there part-time from 2 pm to 5 pm on Mondays to Fridays. Such was her need that if there were no visitors to her back room for coffee each day, she became one of the small band of enthusiastic amateurs who frequented the coffee bars in the High Street of an evening. Her coffee was well known to every company representative, a few officers and occasionally very red and flustered young paper-boys who delivered the evening papers.

One cold, January Saturday night, I was posted to five beat. At about 2.45 am it started to rain, the type of rain which froze as soon as it hit the ground and turned everything into a skating rink. There is a limit to just how long a pair of well-polished leather boots will resist penetration by water, usually about three to four hours, and slowly my feet were getting wetter and colder. I had not brought out my rubber over-shoes (they were not issued and therefore contrary to the clothing regulations, but most senior officers turned a blind eye to them) nor any waterproof leggings. These were quite effective if it was raining when you went on duty, but you had no way of carrying them with you, so if it started raining during your tour of duty they were in your locker at the station and your trousers got soaking wet before you could get back. I drew my cape around me over the top of my thick Milton overcoat, as I trudged my way towards the next set of shops in order to shake hands with their door-knobs. Then I heard the clock at St George's Church strike three. That was it; a cup of tea, a smoke and a warm in Charlie's boiler-house.

Increasing my pace, I soon arrived at the top of the stairs leading to the crypt. For security, Charlie always hid the key of the boiler-room door under the lip of a loose stone coffin-lid at the far end of the crypt, so if you wanted to get into the boiler-room you had to get the key first. I pulled my torch from my pocket but my hands were so cold that it fell from my fingers and rattled down the steps. Completely forgetting where I was, I let forth a string of oaths which put me firmly in line for stoking coal-fired boilers for eternity.

Feeling the wall with my hand, I carefully picked my way down the steep, slimy, slippery stone steps. The deeper I went, the darker it became. What little light there had been from the street lights fifty yards away disappeared completely. When I got to the bottom, I was able to feel the sudden change of temperature. I pulled my cigarette-lighter from my pocket, lit it and held it up high as I slowly and very carefully started to walk across the chamber. I had just about reached the middle when the air was filled with a screeching noise and I glimpsed a whitish blur coming straight at my head. Instinctively I ducked, and my hand rushed to draw my only protection, my truncheon. The trouble was that I was holding my lighter in the same hand. It clattered onto the stone floor and went out. It was then that I proved the truth of the old rhyme about creeping into crypts and creeping out again. The only difference was that I ran out as fast as I could up the slippery steps. As I reached the churchyard, there came a familiar sound: twit-a-woo, twit-a-woo.

That three-weeks spell of night duty was freezing cold the whole time, with sleet and snow showers. On the last Sunday night I had chased suspects over gardens, reported a traffic accident, had two insecure shops and all in all was feeling shattered, particularly because for the past week workmen had been laying a new gas main, sewer and electric cables immediately outside the front of our house. Pneumatic drills, heavy lorries and scraping shovels were not exactly sleep-inducing. Worse than that, I was going on to late turn (2 pm to 10 pm) so I had to be back on duty at 1.45 pm. I rushed home to bed at 6 am, hoping that I could get really sound asleep before the workmen started again and that I might just sleep through it all. A loving wife is a wonderful thing to have but did she have to this morning? I must have got to sleep at about 7.30 am as a result of this and a few minutes later the drills started again. I buried my head under the pillows and tried desperately to get some sleep. A few fitful dozes and by noon I surrendered and got up, knowing that I was to get no sleep.

At 1.45 pm I paraded for duty in a trance. "Asking for four hours time off, Sergeant," I said as my number was called.

"No time off today. We have sent aid to "A" Division so we're short."

Slowly I made my way out of the station and to number one patrol on Ryford High Street. Luckily it was a quiet afternoon, with very few people venturing out in the biting wind. Night came with a rush and by four o'clock it was quite dark. I made my way into the station for early refreshments at 5.30 and by 6.30 I was back on the High Street. I felt awful, dead on my feet. I had to sit down before I fell down.

In Ryford High Street stood the New Theatre, one of the leading repertory theatres in the country. Its layout was unusual because it had been built onto the backs of a long row of shops. By managing to purchase two separate shops, leaving three other shops in between, the developers had been able to create a separate entrance out of one, and a combined emergency exit and stage door from the other. As one entered through the booking office into the foyer the theatre opened out in all directions with seating for several hundred. The solid wood emergency exit doors, serving also as stage doors, were situated almost at the end of a long corridor but leaving a thirty-foot dead- end in which were stored the props required for the current production, there literally being no other storage space backstage. This corridor was only lit when there was a performance or rehearsal in progress. The three pairs of double doors which led immediately on to the pavement were of the full-frosted-glass, swinging type, and one of these was never locked, as even in daylight it was impossible to see to the bottom of the corridor. The management therefore felt it was better to leave the door unlocked so that a police officer could check the bottom doors and store rather than just checking the outer doors. Because of this the night duty patrol officer always had a legitimate reason for being inside the corridor. He was also able to sit down on one of the many chairs and have a smoke whilst watching the glass doors. There was no way he could be surprised.

I reached the theatre, turned and looked up and down the High Street. Not a soul in sight. Quickly I slipped through the swing doors and made my way down the corridor. I was not worried about anyone coming out of the stage door because the theatre had been closed for the whole of the previous three weeks whilst it was being redecorated. When I reached the bottom of the corridor I was delighted to see that a settee covered with a dustcloth was placed facing up the corridor towards the street, with a table and two chairs in front of it. I sat down with a sigh of relief. Before long I began to nod off to sleep.

It was just my luck that Bill Evans should be on the same turn and have the same idea about where to take the weight off his feet for five minutes. He slipped through the theatre's swing doors, took his pipe from his pocket and lit it. As he walked down the corridor, he could just make out in the half-light the figure of a policeman in full uniform sound asleep on the settee. Very gently and carefully, Bill lifted the sleeping figure's legs and laid them out on the settee. He then straightened the dustcover so that it completely covered the sleeping policeman. He then crept quietly out into the High Street and continued on his beat.

"There can be no doubt that he was murdered, Inspector," said a loud voice.

"Why are you so sure about that, Sergeant?" said an equally loud voice.

I opened my eyes and blinked. My face was covered by a white cloth, through which was shining a very strong light.

"He has got a knife stuck between his shoulder blades, sir."

Carefully I eased my body. It didn't feel as if I had anything stuck in my back.

"Any suspects lined up yet?"

"No-one specific as yet, sir, but I've got everyone who was here at the time waiting in the dining room."

"Good man."

I lay quite still, trying to work out exactly what was happening

and to gather my thoughts. Was I dead? Is this what being dead was like, being able to hear all the discussions about you but not being able to answer or do anything? But if I was dead, who had stabbed me and why? Then suddenly it hit me: I was alive, very much alive, but I was lying on a settee covered by a dustsheet in the middle of the stage of the New Theatre, Ryford. Then I remembered that the theatre had been closed for redecoration but tonight was the re-opening night. I froze where I was – never has a live corpse been so stiff. What if they remove the cover? What if they find out who I am? After what seemed an age, I heard the curtains close and the ripple of applause. Before I could move, I suddenly felt the settee being pushed from one end. "Blimey, Harry, you'd think this was a real body on 'ere instead of a dummy, wouldn't yer?"

"Stop bleedin' moanin' and push. We need the table and all the chairs next."

"OK, OK, don't go on."

"Right, that'll do. Leave it there. Now for the table. You take that side. One, two, three, lift."

As soon as I could not hear them any more, I threw off the cover and rushed up the corridor out into the High Street. I glanced up at the clock above Samuels the jewellers – 8.50 pm. I needed to get somewhere out of sight very quickly to compose myself and have a cigarette to calm my nerves. I quickly crossed the road and slipped down the alleyway between the doctor's surgery and the furrier's shop. Slowly I steadied myself and was able to emerge into the world again. Eventually I booked off duty and went to the locker-room. As I entered it I was just in time to see Bill Evans sticking a large silver star on my locker door.

Angus Macleod, the driver and one of the most esteemed members of the nick, was posted to foot beats. This was a very rare occurrence, because of the small number of qualified Class 1 or 2 police drivers at Ryford. Angus was always pleased to get one of these postings, though, claiming that "it got his insides working again". Strangely, this was not all wrong. There was a malady in those days which I am given to understand prevails even today at those few stations where officers still walk the beat early in the morning. You would never find its name in any medical dictionary, nor would a doctor put it on a certificate, although he would be well aware of its symptoms. It was known to all and sundry in the police force as "early turnitis". It invariably struck at some time between 6.30 and 7 am, always when you were furthest away from any place of relief. Its symptoms were always the same: sudden strange rumblings and griping pains in the stomach, with an almost immediate desire to find the nearest toilet at the fastest possible speed. The next time you happen to be out at that time of the morning and see a policeman, have a good look to see if he is walking with fast, short steps and a very set expression on his face; if he is, you can guarantee that he is yet another sufferer of the dreaded "early turnitis". Should you have a rather perverse sense of humour, you could always stop him for directions to somewhere and then ask him to repeat them for you to ensure that you have got them right.

So Angus was well pleased, and he had completed a whole week of early turn without being posted back to the wireless car. He was now on his way into the station for his 6.30 pm refreshment on his first tour of late turn. He turned the corner into East Street and as he did so he could not believe his eyes. There, parked in the narrowest part of the roadway about two feet away from the kerb, was a left-hand-drive, white Cadillac Eldorado 5.4 litre convertible. It had some strange Arabic hieroglyphics on the number-plate and a small but very prominent Corps Diplomatique insignia mounted on the boot-lid. In the driver's seat was a large man dressed in full Arab head-dress and robes. The two-way traffic slowly filtered its way past the obstruction with one or two of the bus drivers telling the Arab gentleman exactly what they thought of him.

Angus reached the car and immediately said, "Ye canna park your car there, sir."

As he said it, the Arab thrust a map and a piece of paper under Angus's nose. "Pleeese, I speeke the Inglish little peece, where pleeese get 'otel?"

Angus looked at the map and was amazed to see that it was of Paris. He then read the paper on which was typed: Carrington House Hotel, Brookmill Road, Deptford, London. Angus gasped out loud in dismay.

Now anyone who has heard Angus speak more than one sentence in his broad Scots accent would be left in no doubt that he, too, could only "speeke the Inglish little peece". So what the outcome of Angus's and the Arab gentleman's conversation was likely to be was anyone's guess, especially with a map of Paris and the address of one of South London's leading doss-houses. Another problem for poor Angus was that the rush-hour traffic was beginning to tail back in either direction. The police Instruction Book clearly stated that if an officer was dealing with a driver of any vehicle which was causing unnecessary obstruction, he should ask the driver to move the vehicle to a more convenient position to avoid aiding and abetting an offence. So Angus politely asked the Arab to move further down the road. "No! No! No! Where pleeese get 'otel?" came the insistent request.

Angus then hit on the idea that if he walked further down the road to where it widened, then the Arab would follow. Why is it that the British firmly believe that all foreigners who cannot speak English are also slow-witted and profoundly deaf? "YE! FOLLOW ME! UNDERSTAND?" he shouted at the Arab. So saying, he marched off down the street. When he had gone about twenty-five yards, he turned to see if the car was following him. As he turned, the Arab walked straight into him. "Nay, laddie, YOU BRING CAR!" So saying, Angus took hold of the Arab by the arm to take him back to the car.

"Me no do wrong, no arrest, me diplo-diplo-ma-tik im-im-im-un-itity!" screamed the Arab.

Angus let go immediately and walked back to the car, the Arab following closely behind him. When Angus reached the car he opened the driver's door and indicated with his hand that the other should get back into the car. Once the Arab had done so, Angus turned over the map and drew a very rough plan of the main roads to Deptford. He then drew a signboard with the word "Lewisham" on it. He handed it to the Arab and then pointed up the road. He made as if he had a steering wheel in his hands and said, "Brmm, brmm."

The Arab nodded his head up and down very slowly, started the car and drove off without another word. Angus shrugged his shoulders and was just about to start walking again when a little boy of about two years old tugged at his trouser leg. "Brmm, brmm," said the two-year-old, and offered Angus a dinky car.

"Thank ye, no, wee laddie. I've got me a big brmm, brmm."

Angus reached the station and booked in for his refreshments. "Why are you late, Angus?" enquired the Station Officer.

"I've bin sorting oot a wog diplomat who thought I'd arrested him."

"A likely story," came the reply.

"It's true, I tell ye." So saying, Angus went upstairs to the canteen. After he had completed his refreshment period, he booked out and was making his way back to his beat when he was surprised to see the white Cadillac drive slowly past him in the direction of the nick. The daft sod, he canna follow some simple directions, Angus thought to himself. He continued on his way, murmuring about foreigners.

I had just been about to book out from my grub when the Station Officer, Sergeant Tom Price, said, "Kenyon, the Section Sergeant and the Duty Officer are tied up with a charge at Hardborough. It's not too busy, so you look after the front office while I have my grub. If there's anything you can't handle, 'phone the canteen and I'll come down, but remember – I don't like being disturbed when I'm eating."

As he got up from the typewriter and left the front office, I found myself in charge. I sat down at the large imposing desk and leaned

back, hands behind my head. I then read every piece of paper I could find lying around the office. Suddenly I stopped myself and realised that I was becoming what is known in the police as a "tray rat": in other words, someone who would go out of their way to search and read reports and other papers in senior officers' in and out trays. I went back to the desk and sat down again. I was just unable to resist the temptation. I glanced all around me to make certain that there was no one in the charge-room who could see me through the glass panel. Then I leaned back and put my feet up on the edge of the desk. Boy, it felt good! There was no doubt about it: although I had no one to order about, authority had gone to my head.

I was just about to become completely decadent and light a cigarette when I heard the sound of the outer front door of the station open and close. I quickly put my cigarette back into its packet and sat correctly at the desk. Grabbing hold of a pen, I threw open a book and bent forward, apparently writing. There came a tapping on the door of the front office. Without looking up I called out, "Come in." The door opened and then closed and I was aware that someone had entered and was standing at the counter. "I won't keep you a moment," I said, apparently just finishing an entry in the book. The fact that I had just noticed that it was upside-down made no difference to my sense of power and importance.

Putting down the pen, I looked up and said, "Can I help you?" There, standing in front of me at the counter, was an olive-skinned man in his thirties, dressed in full Arab costume. As I watched, his right hand reached in front of him and grasped the jewelled hilt of a dagger. The jewels flashed in the light as his hand moved with incredible speed. The curved blade thudded into the top of the counter, point-first. There it stopped, still firmly gripped by its owner. I pushed the chair back in alarm and jumped to my feet. Before I could say or do anything, the man said very slowly and deliberately, "I kill po-lice-man who rape my daughter."

"I'm sorry, sir, would you repeat that?" I faltered, playing for time to see what was going to happen next. At the same time I put my right hand in my trouser pocket and gripped the top of my truncheon just in case.

"I see top po-lice-man. Who de-file my daughter? I have one-two-three-four wives and one-two sons and one-two-three-four-five-six daughters. Old one is sixteen and have big ... How you say ...?" indicating a very large-chested young lady.

I resisted the temptation to be frivolous as even I could see that this was serious. "Breasts," I said.

"Yes, that is the word, tits! She meet po-lice-man from here, this morning. Very big man with strange voice. He foreigner like me, I think. From Scotland, I think. He rape her. I kill."

I gaped. "Yes sir. I understand. If you will wait a moment I will call the Sergeant."

"Him no good, see top po-lice-man," came the reply.

"Just a minute, sir," I said, picking up the telephone handset. "Canteen, please. Sergeant Price, please, very urgent. Will you come down to the front office immediately, Sarge?"

"What is it? It had better be good!"

"It's good all right, Sarge. You'll never believe it."

"OK. On my way." Within a minute Tom Price came through the door into the front office. "Right, what's all this about," he said, immediately followed by a "Jesus Christ!" as he saw the dagger still stuck in the top of the counter. "You all right, Kenyon?"

"Yes thanks, Sarge. This gentleman reckons that he is going to kill the policeman who raped his daughter. What's more, he's just described Jock Macleod. He wants to see top po-lice-man."

"Anything else?" Tom Price enquired.

Bloody hell, I thought, wasn't that enough to be going on with? "No Sarge, that's all. I thought I had better call you," I replied.

"Now sir," said the Sergeant, turning to the Arab. "What exactly is it you want to report?"

"Po-lice-man rape my daughter. I see top po-lice-man."

"Yes sir, but before I call him I must have your name and address and all the details, you understand?"

"Yes, I understand. My name is Abdul Kalif. I am secretary to Jordan Ambassador. Me diplo-diplo-ma-tik im-im-im-un-itity. I have one-two-three-four wives and one-two sons and one-two-three-four-five-six daughters. Old one have big tits." So saying, he let go of the hilt of the dagger and indicated a very large, curvaceous female outline with both hands. As he did this, Tom Price dived for the dagger and removed it from out of the top of the counter.

Before anyone could say anything else, the charge-room door was flung open and Inspector Frank Hillier, alias "General Custer", stormed into the front office.

"Whose bloody great white car is that outside the front of the station? It's parked on the yellow lines, half on and half off the pavement. Kenyon, find out who it belongs to and get it moved and report them for being in a restricted street and obstruction. What's all this about, then?"

"It's all very complicated, sir," said Tom Price. "Right, Kenyon, no need for you to hang around, get back to your beat. It's down to Mr Hillier now, lad."

"Yes Sarge, but I ..."

Tom Price broke in. "On your way, lad."

I booked out and left the station. There outside, just as "General Custer" had described, was a large white Cadillac Eldorado 5.4 litre convertible with strange Arab hieroglyphics on the number-plate and a small but very prominent Corps Diplomatique insignia mounted on the boot-lid. It was parked half on and half off the pavement on the yellow line, facing the on-coming traffic and without lights. Knowing that I would be wasting my time reporting the driver because of diplomatic immunity, I continued on my way.

At about 9.30 pm I noticed the Superintendent's private car come up the High Street, travelling towards the nick. I saluted as it went by and received an acknowledgement. I made my way slowly towards the station, thinking about the Arab. There was something about him which kept on nagging at the back of my mind. I couldn't put a finger on it, but there was something. As I got to the station, the front door was thrown open and the Arab ran down the steps and jumped into the Cadillac. "I wait too long, see daughter in London hospital. No see Commander. Ambassador telephone Home Secretary." With this he started the car, bounced it down the kerb and drove off at a fast speed without any lights on.

Two days later my wife and I were waiting at Dover Ferry Port to meet relatives coming home from holiday. We had arrived early and were sitting in the buffet having a cup of tea. "I say, Dick, isn't that Bill Evans over there?" said Janet. "Over there on the dockside, shaking hands with that man in the big American car."

I looked out of the window and sure enough, there was the same white Cadillac Eldorado 5.4 litre convertible. "Come on," I said and rushed out of the buffet onto the dockside. "Hi there, Bill. Fancy meeting you here."

"Good Lord, you!" said Bill in surprise. "This is my uncle," he went on, indicating the driver of the Cadillac, who was a small, thin Englishman of about fifty-five. "He works for the Jordanian Royal Family. What do you think of the car, eh? Comes with the job. Mind you, he has to drive it right across Europe to get back to work."

We took our leave of Bill and his uncle and went to continue our wait for our relatives. Suddenly my wife said, "Hasn't Bill got a lovely golden tan? It really makes his blue eyes stand out, doesn't it?"

Blue eyes! That was what had been nagging at the back of my mind. Who ever saw an Arab with blue eyes?

CHAPTER 14

As the end of my two years as a probationer approached, I felt that I was growing in confidence. I had a long way to go before I could match the wisdom and experience of men like "Dusty" Miller and Sergeant Tom Price, but I was no longer the wet-behind-the-ears new boy who had walked into Ryford nick for the first time some twenty months earlier. My application for a transfer to dog-handler training at the end of my probationer period was nestling in Superintendent Banford's tray and I had every reason to expect that I was close to fulfilling my long-held ambition. First, though, I was to gain experience in handling a very different kind of animal. It was one of those nights: dull and overcast, with occasional patches of quite dense fog. I peered out of the wireless car windscreen into the fog. "Where exactly are we?" I asked Ted Brewer, who was driving.

"Oh, we're on Axehurst Common, Heading towards Axehurst nick. If this gets any thicker, we'll park up for a while. No sense in charging around if we don't ..." His voice trailed off. "What the bloody hell is that?" he shouted as he slammed on the brakes.

I extricated myself from under the dashboard, pulled myself back into my seat and peered out of the window. "What's what?" I said. "I can't see anyth... I don't believe it!" There, just visible in the headlamps, was the side view of a full-grown Indian elephant.

"Go on, then! You want to be a dog-handler. Go and handle that," said Ted.

"You must be joking. What do I know about elephants?"

"Never mind what you know or don't know, we've got to get it out of the road. Go on, I'll keep the headlamps on it."

"Thanks for nothing," I said as I climbed out of the car, closed the door quietly and slowly, very slowly, edged my way towards the massive beast. "Nice Jumbo, come along then, nice Jumbo," I tried rather timidly. Slowly the elephant turned his head and put out his trunk towards me. Instinctively I drew back, but I was too close and the trunk gently took hold of my arm. "There's a nice Jumbo. What are you doing out here? Come on, old girl, let's lead you off the road." I tried to pull my arm with the elephant attached towards the grass verge. Slowly the beast followed me. "Stay there, Jumbo. Don't run away." I said and returned to the car. "What are we going to do with it?" I enquired of Ted.

"Well, it's a stray animal, and as such should be taken to a pound where it should be lodged until such time as the owner collects it. The nearest pound is Axehurst nick, which is two miles away."

"I'm not walking that distance with it holding onto my arm," I replied. "We must find another way." There was what I was searching for, a length of string about ten feet long, in the corner of the boot of the car. I pulled it out and unwound it. "That should do," I said. Slowly I approached the elephant again, which by this time was peacefully engaged in uprooting small bushes. "Here Jumbo,

Jumbo, be a nice Jumbo," I said reassuringly. Jumbo took no notice at all. I returned to the wireless car. "Here, Ted, what you got for grub tonight?"

"Tomato sandwiches and an apple, why?"

"Give me the apple."

"Not bloody likely."

"If I don't have something to tempt it with, we'll be here all night."

"All right then, but what have you got for grub?"

"Fish-paste sandwiches and somehow I don't think it will like them," I replied. I took the apple, cut it into several pieces and put all the pieces into my pocket except one. Yet again I approached the elephant. "Here, Jumbo, nice Jumbo, would you like some apple then?"

The elephant turned its head and took the piece of apple. Now that I had got its attention, things became easier. As it stood there, I crept forward and tied the string onto its short right-hand tusk. "Come on then, old girl. Let's go for walkies."

Slowly the elephant began to respond to the tugging of the string. Once she had got the message, she at last started moving. "Tell you what Ted, there's no way I'm going to walk to Axehurst. Stop for a second so I can jump in the back and hold the string through the open window." This I did, and the strange procession slowly made its way towards Axehurst.

After nearly an hour and a half, the lights of Axehurst police station could clearly be seen. By this time I was almost hoarse from talking to the elephant. After I had learned not to hold the string tight, but to let it run loosely between my fingers, there had been no trouble, except for the occasional enforced stops to let the clutch of the car cool. By the time we pulled up in the roadway outside the station, I had run out of apple pieces. Axehurst police station was a very old building. It had been there so long that over the years, the road outside had been built up so that one had to descend three steps in order to enter the station proper. For the same reason, the front window-sills of the station were now level with the pavement, and to get into the station yard there was quite a steep slope. Although it covered a large area, Axehurst never had very many men on duty at any one time: with the exception of the two foot patrols around the village centre, the remainder of the ground was covered by two motor cycle patrols.

I got out of the car and looked around for something to tie

Jumbo's string onto. Nothing was immediately handy so I tied the string to the door-handle of the wireless car and went down the steps to the front office. "All correct, Sergeant. Where do I put the elephant?"

The Station Sergeant looked up from his typing. "Right, thank you, lad. There's tea in the pot. Help yourself."

"Thanks very much, skipper, but where do I put the elephant?"

"Now listen here, lad. I've got too much to do to play silly b–s. If you've got an elephant, fetch it in here."

Jumbo was bored and lonely. She had got used to hearing my voice and was wondering where I had gone. Suddenly she heard my voice coming through the top of the slightly opened window of the station. She turned her head towards the sound. As she did so, the door-handle of the car snapped off. Ted gave a squeal of fright and abandoned the car completely, firmly believing that Jumbo was going to start to turn it over. The elephant's trunk pushed its way through the open window and started to explore the coats which hung on the rack just inside. To her delight she found a packet of sandwiches in a pocket and snorted with pleasure. The sound blasted its way around the front office of the station. The reserve man took one look and disappeared through the hatchway into the

canteen. The Station Officer pushed his chair backwards and stood up all in one movement. As he did so, he caught the typing desk with his jacket buckle and tipped the whole thing over as he came upright. "What the hell is that?" he blurted out.

"As I said, skipper, where do I put the elephant?"

"I just don't believe it. In all my years in the job .... Where the hell did you get it from?"

It took some time, but I finally managed to explain and it was decided that it should be tied up with a rope in the station yard.

"Slip down to the baker's and see if he's got any stale loaves he can let us have," the Station Officer told the reserve man. "You, Kenyon, tie it up in the yard, but make sure it's secure."

"Come on, old girl, let's find you a nice place to rest for a while." Obediently Jumbo followed me down the slope into the yard. Looking around, I found the ideal place to tie her up. I made a noose and put it round her neck and fastened the other end to the iron framework of the cycle-shed. "There, that should hold you, old girl. Now stay there and behave yourself."

I returned to the front office and made out my report, while Ted busied himself making the tea. When he told me it was ready, I called, "Yes, OK, I'm almost finished here." The next second there was the most terrible noise from the station yard. Jumbo had heard my voice and was going to find her friend. The station cycle-shed with its angle-iron supports and corrugated asbestos roof was not going to stop her. One good, hard pull and she took it with her, across the yard and up the slope, only stopping when the whole thing got jammed in the gateway. I rushed outside and calmed Jumbo down before all the noise made her stampede.

While I was making soothing noises to Jumbo, the station telephone rang. Had anyone reported seeing an elephant roaming loose? the caller enquired. Lucy was her proper name and she had escaped from a circus's winter quarters about six miles away. Within the hour, Lucy was loaded onto a lorry and was on her way home, whilst I told the story for the tenth time to the night duty and early turn reliefs at six o'clock. For weeks afterwards it was "Jumbo" Kenyon.

* * *

As well as being prepared for anything which the various duties of a police officer could throw at me, I was also learning to harden my feelings about the human tragedies which are an everyday part of police work. With "Blossom" Trevellyn, I dealt with one case which was not only sad but very, very frightening.

"MP, MP from Oscar Six. Put us back in the green please at 15.07."

"Received, Oscar Six. MP out."

All this meant was that I had told Information Room at New Scotland Yard that we were now free to accept more calls in our area. Green on their master board meant we were available and red meant that we were engaged on a call.

"Oscar Six, Oscar Six from MP. A house named The Hollies, Northlands Road, Ryford. See informant re person of unsound mind. Ends origin MP at 15.09."

"MP, MP from Oscar Six. Message received." I logged the call and Blossom steered the car to the location.

The house was a large Victorian one, standing in about four acres of land, with a long, horseshoe-shaped gravel drive. The car crunched to a halt beside the steps leading to the imposing oak front door. As we got out of the car, the door was thrown open and a maid in black dress and white apron and cap ran down the steps, looking fearfully behind her. We went up the steps and peered into the large hallway. As we did so, we just glimpsed a shadowy figure running up the stairs, carrying a large felling axe. Staggering towards us from the direction of the back of the house came a large middle-aged lady, very pale and shaking violently. We rushed in and steered her to an old- fashioned settle which was in the hall. At that moment the maid returned and said that she would make madam a cup of tea if we could make sure that there was no one in the kitchen. I escorted her to the kitchen and was astonished to find kitchen knives, meat-cleavers and a small hand-axe all protruding from the wood of the back door of the house and showing the rough outline of a body-shape.

"It's her son Ivan. He's home on licence from Barming for a week's holiday. He's OK for a long while and then suddenly he goes completely off his head. He forced her to stand against the door and then threw all those knives and things at her. He should never be let out. He did the same thing last time he was out, about three years ago."

"Where do you think he's gone to?" I asked.

"I should say he's gone to his room. It's right at the top of the servants' wing."

"Right. You make a cup of tea for all of us and I'll see what my mate is up to." I went back to the hall.

"Hi, Dick. Mrs Osborne is a bit shaken but doesn't want to go to hospital. She says she's called the welfare officer, who's on the way. She also asks if we could make certain that her son hasn't hurt himself."

"OK, Blossom. Where do we go?" I enquired.

Having received directions, we set off upstairs and through a maze of corridors until eventually we reached the narrow flight of stairs which led to the very top of the house. As we slowly mounted the stairs, I made sure that Blossom was in front of me. At the top there was a door on the right-hand wall with a very small landing outside. "Try the door then, Bloss," I dared.

Very quietly Blossom put his ear to the door and listened intently. After about a minute he said, "Not a sound. I don't think he's in there."

"Well, the only way to find out is to go in. Go on, try opening the door."

Very gently Blossom took hold of the large brass door-knob and turned it slowly. He then pushed hard against the door. Absolutely nothing happened. There was not the slightest movement. "He's got

something jammed against it. It's not just locked, it's solid. There's no give in it at all."

"Try talking to him and ask him to let you in." I suggested, taking one step down the stairs.

"What's his name again?"

"Ivan," I said.

"Ivan?" Blossom asked incredulously.

"Yes, Ivan. I-V-A-N, Ivan."

"It can't be. No one is called Ivan these days," exclaimed Blossom.

"Get on with it. Ask him to let you in. Go on."

Blossom turned and knocked gently on the door. "Come along, Ivan. We are policemen. We are not going to hurt you. We just want to see if you're hurt or not. Let us in please." I was surprised just how kind and gentle Blossom's beautiful Cornish accent sounded.

We both listened intently, but there was not a sound. After a minute, Blossom repeated his statement. This time there was a sudden movement from inside the room. Then there was a smashing sound and an axe-blade appeared through the top panel of the door. Although I was four steps below Blossom on the stairs, we both reached the comparative safety of the large landing at the bottom of them together.

"What do we do now?" I asked.

"I'm going to telephone the nick and get them to call the duly authorised Mental Health Officer, and also an ambulance. You stay here and talk to him, try to get his confidence," replied Blossom.

"I've got a better idea. I'll go and make the phone call and you talk to him. After all, he knows your voice."

"No way. Look what my voice made him do. You talk to him." So saying, Blossom took off along the corridor.

"Don't take too long," I called after him. Then I returned to the door. "Hello, Ivan, my name is Dick. I am here to help you. Would you like a cup of tea? Elsie the maid is making one. Do you take sugar?" I said quietly from the stairs, making sure that I kept away from the landing immediately in front of the door, which still had the axe-head sticking through it. "Come along, Ivan, I won't hurt you. Wouldn't you like a nice cup of tea? It won't take any time at all to get you one if you would like one. Come on, Ivan, open the door for me."

Suddenly I heard a movement inside the room, then there was the sound of a really heavy piece of furniture being dragged across the floor. There was a click and the door swung open about two inches.

"Thank you very much, Ivan. Now you go and sit down on something as far away from the door as possible and I'll come in to see you." There was the sound of footsteps and the creak of a bed-spring. Slowly and very carefully, I made my way up the last two stairs and pushed the door open about two feet, easing my truncheon from my pocket at the same time. Nothing happened. I pushed the door open as far as it would go and stepped in.

There on the far side of the room was a single bed against the wall and sitting on it was a small man, less than five feet tall, wearing huge thick-lensed glasses. I thought he was aged about fifteen, but in fact he was almost forty. He just sat there and blinked at me rather like an owl but never said a word. I was talking to him quietly and reassuringly so that he was not frightened, whilst at the same time searching the room with my eyes for any sign of another weapon.

The room was clean, neat and fastidiously tidy. There was nothing out of place and things were laid out with absolute precision. On top of a dressing-table there was a row of ordinary pins, exactly one inch apart with all the points level and placed in descending lengths. On the end of the bed was a pair of striped pyjamas, folded and placed in such a way that the stripes of the jacket were exactly in line with those of the trousers. As I looked around, I could see there had been a heavy oak chest of drawers against the door. Tentatively I tried to lift one end with one hand. Nothing happened, and from the weight I would have been hard put to lift it with two hands, yet little Ivan had pushed it into place and removed it all by himself.

At that point I heard footsteps on the stairs. Ivan suddenly sat bolt upright. "It's all right, Ivan, it's only me. You know me, don't you? I come and see you in hospital and bring you sweets, don't I?" came a woman's voice.

For the first time Ivan spoke. "Yaas, you do," he said in a high-pitched, squeaky voice.

As she entered the room, the woman said, "You're going to be a good boy now, aren't you, Ivan?"

"Yaas, I am," he replied in the same high-pitched voice.

The woman whispered to me, "I'm the Welfare Officer. He'll be all right now." Without giving me time to answer, she continued in a loud voice, "Elsie has made a nice cup of tea and I've brought some cake. We'll go downstairs and have some, shall we?"

"Yaas, we will." Ivan stood up and limped across the room. It was then that I noticed for the first time that he was wearing a surgical boot on his left leg. Slowly the woman led Ivan downstairs with Blossom and me following a short distance behind.

"Now it's time to go back to the hospital. You're going to be a good boy, aren't you?" asked the woman.

"Yaas, I am."

"He will need his suitcase which is under his bed. Would you go and get it for him please, officer?" the Welfare Officer said to me.

I returned to the bedroom and bent down to retrieve the suitcase from under the bed. As I put my left hand on the bed to steady myself, it touched something cold and a sudden twinge of pain shot up my forefinger. I pulled my hand away quickly and there, half-hidden in a ruck of the bedding where Ivan had been sitting, was a fully opened cut-throat razor. I offered up a silent prayer of thanks.

When I got back to the hall, Ivan was impassively staring at the two ambulancemen undoing the back doors of the ambulance. The duly authorised Mental Health Officer had also arrived. He went over and spoke to them. One of the men entered the ambulance and emerged carrying what looked like a piece of rolled-up canvas. Together all three climbed the steps and came through the door.

"You're going to go back to hospital now, Ivan. You will be a good boy, won't you?" said the Welfare Officer.

A deep voice rumbled from somewhere deep inside Ivan and screamed, "No, I'm bleeding not! I'm not going back to that bloody hole!" It was then that he went berserk, arms and legs flailing everywhere. Two ambulance men, one duly authorised officer, one welfare woman (large size), one mother, one maid and two police officers struggled for nearly twenty minutes to subdue and restrain a man less than five feet tall. His strength was unbelievable.

Eventually Ivan was placed in a straightjacket and driven away in the ambulance. We gathered all the necessary names and addresses and went to Ryford nick, where we had our refreshments and wrote out our reports. Then we booked back on the air, just in time to receive a call to a traffic accident in the High Street. As we got near it became obvious that something serious had happened. London-bound traffic was at a standstill over a mile away. Carefully Blossom weaved his way towards the scene, squeezing between the oncoming traffic and the stationary line. Eventually we got to within 150 yards of the accident. From there we had to walk.

The sight which met our eyes was a shambles. Almost at a right angle to the pavement and completely blocking the road was an articulated lorry that had jack-knifed. Entangled in the front near-side wheel of the tractor unit was what was left of a small Austin saloon. Embedded in the back of that was a black Citroen with French number-plates on.

Poking out from under the centre of the lorry's fully laden trailer was about two feet of the front of a Lea Francis sports car which was apparently undamaged until one looked for the windscreen. Wrapped around a lamp-standard was an AJS motor cycle, the rider of which was hanging half in, half out of a shop window which had once been fitted with plate glass. There was also the usual horde of morbid on-lookers, the people who are more of a hindrance than anything else at an accident where there is death or destruction; none of them, of course, saw anything if asked to be a witness.

"Right, Dick. You go back to the car, get on to the Information Room and ask for two ambulances, more police assistance, fire brigade and heavy lifting gear," instructed Blossom. I did as he said and, after passing the message, returned to the scene. "See if you can find any witnesses, get a quick statement from them and then take the particulars of the people in the Citroen," Blossom told me.

"Did anybody see what happened?" I shouted at the crowd.

This enquiry met with the usual downturned eyes, and mumbles of "Not me" from several different mouths.

"Come on, someone must have seen something, surely?" I shouted.

This time my request brought a response from a young man who was obviously not yet old enough to have learnt that as a member of a crowd at an event like this, you can stand and watch but you never see anything. "Right, come over here," I said.

The young man came and so did half of the crowd, who gathered round to hear the gory details. I ordered the crowd back, took the man's name and address and listened to his version. We established that he had had jellied eels at the pie and mash shop for lunch and that he had seen the accident when his manager had sent him out again to find a bookie's runner to place a bet on a horse running at Ascot that afternoon. The motor cyclist had been travelling towards London when a small boy had run out into the road chasing a tennis ball, immediately in front of him. The rider had swerved to his offside to avoid the boy, lost control and smashed into the lamp-post, then he had flown across the pavement, head-first through the shop window. Like most motor cyclists in those days, he was not wearing a crash-helmet. The lorry had been coming from London when the driver saw the boy and the motor cycle coming across the road in front of him. He had swerved to his offside to avoid them and the trailer had jack-knifed, pushing the whole unit across the road. The Austin, travelling towards London, had had no chance of avoiding the tractor unit and had smashed into the front wheel. The Citroen had run into the back of the Austin. The Lea Francis sports car, which had a man driving and a woman passenger, had apparently just started to accelerate to overtake the lorry as it swerved and jack-knifed. The Lea Francis had disappeared under the side of the lorry, coming to a halt jammed underneath it. From the screams and shouting coming from under the trailer, the driver was very much alive.

Thanking the witness, I turned my attentions to the driver of the Citroen, a man of about forty-five with a huge, bushy beard. He was sitting sideways on the front seat of the remains of his car, with his feet on the roadway and his head in his hands, his elbows resting on his knees. As I neared him, he jumped up and started to wave his arms around, at the same time jabbering away at me in French. Now I had gone to a technical school where we were taught engineering, building or art. The learning of such things as languages was for those "namby-pamby" lot who went to the grammar school. My entire French vocabulary consisted of "Oui" and "Non".

"What – is – your – name?" I asked very slowly, emphasising each word in turn.

The reply came in the form of about a hundred words which were completely unintelligible to me.

"Yes, but do – you – speak – English?"

"Ah yes. Small piece. Small words," came the reply.

Thank goodness, I thought. Maybe I can get through to him. "What – is – your –name?" I asked again, very slowly and deliberately. Once again, the reply was a stream of unintelligible French. After this pantomime had been repeated twice more, the situation was saved by a lady in the crowd, who stepped forward and said, "I speak French. Can I translate for you?" I could have kissed her, not because she was very beautiful but because she could speak French as well: a rare find in an area where they speak their own particular South London brand of Cockney.

In a very few minutes I had all the information I needed and was in the process of thanking the woman when suddenly she went very pale, then slowly and quite gracefully collapsed unconscious onto the pavement. Before I could do anything, I felt a tapping on my right trouser-leg. Looking down and slightly behind me I saw a small girl aged about four. She was wearing a blue dress, the colour of which almost matched her eyes, and her blonde hair was done in a pony-tail. " 'Ere y'are, mister. You'll want this bit, won't yer?" she said, handing me the remains of a woman's head, which she was holding by the hair. "Found it under the back of the lorry, I did," she added and skipped away back across the road. She disappeared into the crowd, which had suddenly diminished in size.

Blossom and I eventually cleared up the mess, and saw the dead and injured into ambulances and got the traffic moving again. It was two hours after our normal booking-off time when we finally got back to the station. "Dusty" Miller was there, chatting to the Station Sergeant, and he listened as we recounted the story of our eventful shift. Then he nodded and said, "Well done, lad. You'll make a proper policeman yet." Those few words meant that I was accepted. I had passed the stiffest probation period of the lot, and most importantly, I was accepted and respected by my peers.

CHAPTER 15

The large black limousine, complete with pulled blinds around the passenger compartment, slid to a halt in Ryford High Street, double-parking in the process. I looked up the road and immediately noticed the car, which stood out like a sore thumb. How dare anyone even think of such a thing when I was on duty, posted to the High Street? After all, I was beginning to earn myself a bit of a reputation when it came to parking. Wasn't it me who reported the Superintendent's wife for parking on a yellow line? And it was me who was going to report the Chairman of Magistrates' daughter before she started giving birth right there in the street. There was no way the driver of this car was going to get away with it.

As I approached the car, the chauffeur got out and stood beside the nearside passenger door, looking up the alleyway between the shops towards the house at the end.

"Sorry, mate, you can't park there," I said in a pleasant enough voice.

"There's no choice, officer. I can't 'ave my governor walking a hundred yards down the road to get his car, can I?" protested the chauffeur.

"Look, mate, I don't care who your governor is. He can be the Prime Minister of England for all I care. You can't double-park there," I said in a slightly more officious voice.

Just as I said it, a tall, grey-haired man, dressed in a black crombie overcoat, stepped from between the cars towards the limousine. The chauffeur opened the door and saluted. The tall man said, "Quite right too, officer, even if I am the Prime Minister. Right Charles. Off you go, as quickly as possible."

"Very good, sir," said Charles.

I was left with my right arm almost into a salute, my mouth partly open and my eyes staring in disbelief, as the limousine sped away carrying Harold Macmillan to his next appointment at a local Conservative party headquarters.

"Why wasn't I told?" I demanded in the reserve room back at Ryford station.

"You should have been. I gave the message to Bill Evans to give to you."

"Well, I never got it. What a bloody fool I made myself look," I grumbled.

Just then, the notorious Bill Evans entered the room, laughing all over his face. "All set for tomorrow then, Dick?" he asked.

"I suppose so, but I've a good mind not to turn up," I said sullenly.

The next day was the day that Bill was to marry the voluptuous Shirley Long. Strangely, in spite of his peculiar humour, Bill had managed to get eight of us police colleagues to agree to form a guard of honour. It was more the promise of free beer and food afterwards than our friendship with Bill which had caused us to agree, as we had all been on the wrong end of Bill's practical jokes at one time or another. I walked down to the church with Ted Brewer, Angus Macleod and "Blossom" Trevellyn. The only absentee was Tony Yorke, Bill Evans' favourite victim for his pranks, who had recently been transferred to another division without carrying out his frequent promise to get even with Bill for all that he had suffered.

The church was the oldest in Ryford and it presented an idyllic surrounding for the wedding. All had gone according to plan. It was warm, but with a slight breeze – just enough for the bride's veil to be moved sufficiently to reveal tantalising glimpses of her ample appointments. As she arrived, the whole congregation, including myself and the seven other guards of honour, rose. After the bridal party had passed us at the rear of the church and were proceeding down the aisle, I glimpsed a rather strange-looking figure in a cape and top hat standing in the porch of the church. The service started and I dismissed him from my mind.

"If any person knows of any just cause or impediment why these two persons should not be joined together in holy matrimony, let them speak now or forever hold their peace," the vicar was saying.

"STOP! STOP THE WEDDING!" boomed out a voice from the back of the church.

A gasp came from the congregation as they all turned to stare. There, running down the aisle towards the bride and groom, came an immaculately dressed figure wearing a morning suit and a black cloak with a red lining, carrying a top hat, white gloves and a silver-knobbed cane. I also noticed that the figure appeared to be wearing very heavy make-up.

"THE GROOM IS ALREADY MARRIED AND I CAN PROVE IT!" the man shouted as he reached Bill Evans and grabbed

him by the shoulder. He thrust his face forward so that it was about a foot away from Bill's, then he stopped, gasped and said, "Oh my god! Sorry! Wrong wedding!" With that, he turned and ran up the aisle, uttering maniacal laughter.

The church was in an uproar. Shirley was in an unconscious heap on the floor. Bill looked as if he were going to pass out at any moment. The bride's mother was standing on the pew, screaming. The best man was doing his best to molest the hysterical bridesmaid. The vicar was trying unsuccessfully to restore some semblance of calm. The ushers ran around, not quite knowing what they were doing. Eventually things quietened down and after a half-hour delay, the wedding ceremony was completed without any further interruptions.

Bill's brother, John, was best man and was responsible for reading out the telegrams at the reception. "May all your troubles be little ones, with love from Auntie Ada and Uncle George." Always very original with their jokes, aren't they? The next one, from Ryford main post office, is addressed to Bill alone. It reads: "No one deserves it more than you," and it's signed "the caped avenger."

Who this "caped avenger" was no one ever found out, but some weeks later Janet and I went to see a performance at the New Theatre. As we waited for the curtain to rise, I noticed in the programme the line "Costumes and make-up by Susan Yorke." A coincidence? Or did Tony Yorke enlist his sister's expert help to give Bill Evans' his final come-uppance?

* * *

"PC R. Kenyon, with reference to your application to be considered for Dog-Handling Duties you are warned to attend a selection interview on .... You are reminded that the successful applicant must, as close as possible, meet with the requirements as laid out in General Orders and in Her Majesty's Stationery Office Publication "Police Dogs, Training and Care". Reply direct to this office when the officer has been informed."

It had happened! At long last I was on the first rung of the ladder to my ambition. I quickly obtained a copy of the HMSO publication and eagerly searched for the relevant chapter. It read as follows :

DOG HANDLERS______________________________

1. The careful selection of men suitable for training as dog-handl-

ers is vital to the successful employment of dogs for police purposes. At all stages of training and operational use, the handler and the dog work as a team, often with the minimum of supervision. The selection of suitable personnel for training is, therefore, no less important than the careful selection of dogs.

2. Men to be considered for training as dog-handlers must be sound, experienced policemen whose mental alertness, equable temperament and willingness to persevere are above average. The nature of the training and subsequent operational work calls for a high standard of physical fitness.

3. Previous experience with animals may well be an advantage but the lack of it is not necessarily a disqualification in the case of an otherwise suitable officer. It is important, however, that a handler should have a forceful character with a determination to succeed and a cheerful disposition which will be reflected subsequently in the behaviour of his dog. A handler of a brusque or nagging disposition will confuse and may easily ruin a dog.

4. In cases where a police dog is to be kennelled at the home of the handler, serious consideration should be given to the home background and, in particular, to home ties. It is essential to ensure that no disruption of the family life of the handler will result, and that the general atmosphere of the household is placid. Adequate kennelling facilities must be available in a position where interference with and disturbance of the dog is minimised.

5. The devotion of the handler to the dog and to duty must be without question: the former will ensure a mutual confidence and respect which will be shown in the dog's attitude to work, and the latter is an operational necessity more especially in areas where the number of police dogs is small.

6. The technical ability of a handler can only be really judged after he has been allocated a dog for a "Familiarisation Course", or when he commences full training.

The more I read, the more I decided it had all been a big mistake and I should never have applied in the first place. After all, my escapades in the previous two years suggested there might be more minuses than pluses. In spite of this initial feeling, it did not take me long to assure myself that I was better than the rest of the applicants. Never for one moment did it occur to me that if I was successful, it could be because I was the best of a bad lot.

As it was, by a strange quirk of fate I never really knew where I stood. There were two other applicants for the vacancy at Ryford, both of whom had considerably more service than I had. Before the interview, one had withdrawn his application after his wife learnt about it – the requirement that "the general atmosphere of the household is placid" debarred his application once she had made her views known. The second, unfortunately for him, was discovered by the Section Sergeant one late turn, helping the landlord of the King's Arms to empty his barrel of best bitter whilst still on duty. This left me.

I went for the interview, answered all the questions to the best of my ability and was able to put the icing on the cake by telling the selection board that the day before I had had an arrest of a particularly troublesome daytime housebreaker. Not showing much skill in the art of man-management, the board left it two weeks before telling me that I had been accepted and was to go on the very next available course. In spite of the state of my finances, Janet and I had a celebratory dinner that night.

Within the next week I was warned to attend Lambeth stores to collect my dog- handling equipment. This included such items as one lead, leather, dog (I always knew they were artificial); one galvanised dustbin with lid (the use of which escaped me at the time but which I found out later was for storing dog biscuits in as it was mice-proof); one brush, dandy (was I being allocated a "gay" dog?); one scrim cloth; one gallon of disinfectant; one bar of household soap and one scrubbing brush (or even a dirty dog?). There were several more items of additional uniform and dog-handling equipment but by far the most impressive was one kennel, wooden. When this was erected in the garden of our block of flats I was worried that I would not be able to stop the local council from requisitioning it as a halfway house for a homeless family. It was in fact to prove one of the most useful items of equipment that I was issued with, but not as a dog's living quarters.

Now that I was issued with all the equipment I could hardly wait to start a course, but wait I had to. Eventually, six months later, I was warned to start a dog-handling course at the Dog Training Establishment, Keston, near Biggin Hill in Kent. On the first day I was collected by a kennel van from Ryford station. These vans were converted two-tonners which had wire-mesh kennels fitted in two rows of three on top of one another at the rear of the van and two bench-seats, one down either side, for the handlers. The vans were garaged at Lambeth each night and made a circular tour, collecting handlers and dogs in the morning and dropping them off in the late afternoon. This avoided handlers and their dogs travelling on public transport, not to mention the 2½-mile walk to the training establishment from the closest point any public transport reached. I was dressed in wellington boots and dark blue overalls and the weather was one of those beautiful Indian Summer days we so often get in September in England, with the temperature in the upper sixties by 9 am. This, coupled with excitement and apprehension, meant that I had beads of perspiration on my forehead as I lined up with the five other members of the course. The only one of them that I vaguely knew was Charlie Tope from St John's on Ryford sub-division. Five of us were from the Metropolitan Police whilst the sixth was from the City of London force.

"I'm your course instructor. My name is Sergeant Stan Conway. For the next thirteen weeks I am going to be the thorn in your side and hopefully, at the end of that time we will pass out six trained dogs and handlers. This morning we are not going to start in the normal way. Both of our kennelmen have gone sick and we are going to use you to exercise and muck-out all the dogs in the kennels. They are not all trained and some of them will end up being handled by you, so take care and if you are not certain, ask. Here is a training lead each." Sergeant Conway handed each of us a leather lead which had a clip at either end and two metal loops positioned in such a way that the lead could be used at three different lengths; at its longest it was about five feet. "If you use it doubled, you have a loop which you can place your arm or leg through should you need both hands free to do anything whilst you have a dog on the end. If it is a big dog, make an extra loop round your ankle so that he can't pull it from under your feet, like this." He demonstrated exactly what he meant. "Now you! What's your name?" he said, pointing at me.

"Kenyon, Sergeant," I replied, quite proud that I had been picked out so early. The fact that I was standing on the end of the line closest to him had nothing to do with it.

"OK, Kenyon, a special job for you to start with. In the last kennel in this row you will find a goat. Yes, that's right, a goat! We have it tethered out in the training field so that the dogs under training get used to there being other animals around and they learn that they must not attack them. About half-way down the field is a metal stake driven into the ground. On it is a metal chain. Get the goat, put your lead on its collar which it wears all the time, walk it down to the chain, clip the chain to the collar, take off your lead and come back and clean out one of the kennels, OK?"

"Yes, Sergeant. I think so," I answered, slightly disappointed.

"Good. Away you go then, lad."

I walked away, feeling rather upset that the others had got dogs to deal with and I'd got a goat. As I entered the kennel compound the whole place exploded into a crescendo of barking dogs. The kennels were brick-built and measured approximately twelve feet by twelve feet. At the back was a sleeping area which was wooden-floored and raised clear of the concrete base. The sides were of solid single-brick wall about ten feet high and the front had an eight-foot-high metal-framed chain-link gate, a low brick wall and then chain-link fencing on top of it. There were eight of these kennels on each side of a large space approximately a hundred feet square, with all the kennels facing inwards. There were additional kennels backing onto those on one side.

As I walked slowly towards the last kennel and reached a position where I was able to see into it, I was amazed to come face to face with the largest billy goat I had ever seen in my life. The whole look of this massive animal was one of malevolence. Its horns were nearly two feet long, curving back over its head. It stood pawing the ground with its right front leg, tossing its head up and down and from side to side. It only needed to strike sparks with its hoof, snort smoke from its nostrils and smell of sulphur and brimstone, and I would have been convinced that I was being faced by a reincarnation of Beelzebub himself. As it was to turn out, this is what I am convinced he was. In fact, during the whole of his service in the police dog section, nothing he did ever changed my mind.

Gingerly I approached the kennel gate and slid back the bolt. Then, slowly, I opened the gate just wide enough to slide through, expecting this massive animal to charge me at any moment. As I entered, he stopped pawing the ground and tossing his head. He glared at me with large, bloodshot, unblinking eyes, then slowly and deliberately he walked towards me. I held out my hand with the lead-clip open, ready to catch it on the beast's collar when he was close enough. I realised I must stay close to the gate and not let him get between me and my only route to safety. He came to within three feet of me and stopped. I scanned his neck in the hope that I would be able to see the brass loop on his collar on which to clip the lead. Brass loop? What a hope! All I could see was a hairy neck. Slowly I put out my hand and touched the brute's neck. He did not flinch, my confidence grew and I took a step nearer so that I was not stretching to find the collar. Immediately I took this step, I realised that I had done wrong, but before I could correct it, the billy moved like lightning and placed himself between me and the gate.

As I looked at the animal, I caught sight of a small group of people standing in the centre of the compound, all looking in my direction and smirking. Obviously I was to be the poor unfortunate novice who was to provide the permanent staff with some entertainment. For some reason this infuriated me. I stepped forward, grabbed the goat's neck, searched with my hand and found the collar and the brass "D" ring, clipped the lead onto it and jerked hard on the lead. As I did so, the goat came away from the gate. Immediately I carried through my advantage, opened the gate fully and stepped out, dragging a startled goat into the compound.

My advantage lasted only a very few seconds before the goat was able to realise what had happened. Immediately he did so, he planted all four feet firmly on the ground and stood fast. Now, having had to listen on many nights to "Blossom" Trevellyn's tales of working heavy horses, I was well aware that if an animal's eyes suddenly picked out something that worries it, nothing in the world will make it move towards it. However, if you turn the animal away from the object and return at a different angle, the animal completely ignores whatever was bothering it and will happily walk on. Using this maxim, I yanked at the goat's head and got it to walk away from the entrance to the field, then I turned and we walked slowly but surely through the entrance and down the field towards the stake and chain. After about ten minutes we reached the end of the chain. Remembering what I had been told, I wrapped the loop of the lead around my leg twice, stood firmly on the lead as well and bent down to pick up the chain from out of the grass.

About fifty yards away, Charlie Tope stopped walking with the second dog he was exercising to roll himself a cigarette. He too dropped the lead to the ground to put his foot through it. In the split second that the lead was not attached to or trapped by part of Charlie, the dog had spotted the goat and rushed towards it, barking and snarling. In a desperate effort to stop the dog, Charlie dived at the end of the lead and ended up face-first in what is officially known

as the exercise patch, but it is known to all as "the shit patch".

The goat was used to this happening. After all, that was what he was kept for, as was a tiny black she-cat who would sit impassively whilst even two or three dogs attacked her; then she would stand up, stretch herself, and suddenly she would dance forward on her back legs, spitting and clawing in a ripping movement, apparently with all four feet. After one such engagement, a dog always had healthy respect for the feline species. The goat reacted in much the same way as the cat: it would wait until the attacking dog got within range and

then charge it, butting it all over the place. I, of course, did not know this at the time and was laughing at poor Charlie's predicament when the next thing I knew was that my left leg shot up in the air and was pulled forward at the same time. The lead tightened around my leg and I fell backwards. The goat set about the dog with a will, particularly as it was not restricted by a chain welded to a stake driven into the ground. All it had was 150 pounds of human, which it was able to drag around wherever it wanted, whilst the human's back and head felt as if it was being pounded by an army of navvies. The goat must have covered a good hundred yards before I eventually managed to free my leg, regain my feet and tether the beast, while Charlie caught the dog.

It was hardly the best start to my service in the Metropolitan Police Dog Section. That service was to extend to twenty happy and fulfilling years, but for the first three months I was known to all and sundry as "Billy"!